MAR 29 1995			
JUN 29 1995			
DEC 19 1995			
DEC 22 1995			
MAY 09 1996			
MAR 25 1999			

The Kids' Book About Parents

Books by Students at
Fayerweather Street School
and Eric E. Rofes

The Kids' Book of Divorce
The Kids' Book About Parents

The Kids' Book About Parents

by Students at
Fayerweather Street School
and Eric E. Rofes

Houghton Mifflin Company *Boston* 1984

Letters to the authors of *The Kids' Book About Parents* should be sent in care of Fayerweather Street School, 74 Fayerweather Street, Cambridge, MA 02138.

Library of Congress Cataloging in Publication Data
Main entry under title:

The Kids' book about parents.

Summary: Thirty-one children, ages eleven to fourteen, from a variety of family situations, address numerous parent-child issues to help other "kids" develop strategies in dealing with parents. Includes sixty-four specific topics such as overprotectiveness, bedtime, gay parents, adoption, sex, and punishment.
1. Parent and child—United States. 2. Parents—United States. [1. Parent and child. 2. Children's writings] I. Rofes, Eric E., 1954– II. Fayerweather Street School. Unit.
HQ755.85.K52 1984 646.7'8 83-49064
ISBN 0-395-35394-7

Printed in the United States of America

v 10 9 8 7 6 5 4 3 2 1

ACKNOWLEDGMENTS

We wish to thank the following people who have helped us with our work on this book: Linda Brown and Madeline Leeds for helping us with copying, typing, telephone calls, advice, and guidance; Martha Older for typing the completed manuscript and for giving a great deal of feedback about the book; Jinnie Spiegler, our student teacher, and Jorie Hunken, our science teacher, for helping with classes and encouraging our work throughout the year; our parents, who trusted us in our work on this book and supported our efforts to discuss difficult personal issues; Helen Rees, our agent, who helped with the development of the book and found us a publisher; Frances Tenenbaum, our helpful editor at Houghton Mifflin; Robenia Myrer Smith, Paula Rofes, David Hocker, and Diane Hocker, who read the manuscript and gave us a lot of important feedback; Marianne and Macy Lawrence for their help with photographs; Jane Pincus for supplying us with parenting books to look over; the parents, teachers, and kids at Fayerweather Street School, who served as models in the photographs; the other kids in our class and at the Fayerweather Street School, who helped us think about all the issues in this book and contributed their ideas and stories to the final manuscript.

CONTENTS

INTRODUCTION: HOW AND WHY WE WROTE THIS BOOK

We are thirty-two kids between the ages of eleven and fourteen from a class called "the Unit" at the Fayerweather Street School in Cambridge, Massachusetts. We come from all kinds of families — some of us live in the traditional nuclear family, some in single-parent families, some in joint-custody situations. All of us have problems with our parents — both typical problems and unusual ones. We wrote this book to help ourselves — and other kids — deal with parents.

There are many books available for parents about raising children, but we don't know of any books for kids that discuss dealing with parents. In the world we live in, we know that kids are no longer happy, simple little people who play in the park all day and do whatever their parents tell them to do. Kids today have to deal with situations within their families — as well as in the outside world — that are sometimes scary and sometimes difficult. In this book, we recognize these issues as being very important in the lives of many American children today.

Some people say that because kids today know about sex, violence, drugs, divorce, and many other things, childhood no longer exists. They say that kids are forced to be adults too early in life, that they have major responsibilities placed on them as early as six and seven years old. We have seen cases where kids have been forced to deal with certain things that are really adult issues and we do know some parents who give their kids too much responsibility when they are still too young. In general, however, we think kids are still kids — even in the 1980s — and that the major change that has taken place is that now everyone is being honest with us about things. People don't hide things from the children very much or try to protect us from reality.

We wrote this book because we think kids need to develop strategies to help them deal with parents. In this book, you will find advice on everything from how to talk your parent into giving you a bigger allowance to how to deal with life in a single-parent home and how to handle an overprotective parent and still have fun. Parents will also enjoy this book and we think that it will help them deal with their children in an honest and caring way.

We started work on this project in September 1982, at the beginning of our school year. Some of us worked on the book all year and some of us just for a few weeks. We started out by making a list of all the topics that we thought should be included and then we spent some time throughout the school year on each topic. Our teacher, Eric Rofes, helped us begin to think about each topic through drama, art, or written exercises. For example, one day he divided us into groups and we made lists of all the foods parents forced us to eat that we didn't like. Then we got back together, looked over the lists, and began to talk about the situation. We then got writing assignments that involved the topic. At the end of the year, Eric took the assignments from all of us and pulled them together into the finished text of the book. We read over each chapter and made corrections, changes, and additions.

Most of us had fun working on this book. We learned a lot from our discussions with other kids about ways to deal with our parents. We think it's a good idea for kids of all ages to get together and talk about the problems they have with their parents, because you can find solutions to your problems or at least understand that you're not the only one with your problem. We hope this book will encourage children — and parents — to look at their relationship with their family and take an active role in making things happier and healthier for everyone.

Nathan ("Nate") Albert
Kecia Albright
David Alperovitz
Jasanne Blanchard
Jesse Blout
Seth Boyd
Caleb Brown
Jake Burlingham
Elizabeth Carr
Jamey Chancey-O'Quinn
Gillian Cohen
Justin Dore
Mike Foreman-Fowler
Kristin Hagen
Jonathan Knight
Joy Koller
Macy Lawrence
Kate Leopold
Kama Lurie
Becca Lynch
Stephen Lynch
Joachim Martin
John McClain
Matt Murphy
Heidi Pinton
Ana Polonsky
Josh Schreier
Andre Shoy
Mindy Sobota
Heather Sparks
Nat Stoddard
Tanya Wasserman

PART I

What Is a Parent?

People We Call Parents

Before we did much work on this book, we talked about what we mean when we talk about "parents." We realized that the kids in our class live in a lot of different family situations — some live with their mothers and fathers, some live with a single parent, some live with a stepparent and a father or mother, some travel back and forth between parents' homes, some live in a household with other adults besides their parents, and some don't live with either their fathers or their mothers.

Through our discussions, we realized that a parent is a person who takes responsibility for the feeding and caring of a child and is the adult to whom the child might go for help and support. We also realized that there are two parts to parenting. The first part is the actual giving of life to the child and the second is raising the child. This distinguishes two kinds of parents: The biological parent is the actual blood relative — the child's mother or father by birth; the guardian parent is the parent who does the actual caring for and nurturing of the child. Sometimes both of these roles are performed by the same person and sometimes by different people.

Those of us who are still living with both of our biological parents in the same household live in what is considered to be the traditional American family, or the nuclear family. Those of us who live with only one of our biological parents — due to divorce, separation, or the death of a parent — live in a single-parent home (unless, of course, our parent has remarried or moved in with another person). In some cases, our parent has remarried and we have a stepparent living with us. The stepparent may be an example of a person who is not the biological parent, yet is the guardian parent. Some children are adopted or, for some other reason, do not live with either of their biological parents. In this situation, the person they live with is their guardian parent.

We talked about how many people each of us considers to be our parents. Jesse considers three people to be his parents — his father, his mother, and Linda Brown, a family friend. His father is a "parent in blood" and plays a part in bringing him up and so does his mother. These are the two people he loves most in the world. Linda Brown is extremely close to Jesse and is like another mother to him. Jesse also has a stepmother, Stephanie, whom he thinks of as a "half-parent" because he doesn't think she could take the place of his mother.

Josh wrote, "I consider myself to have four parents: my immediate biological parents and my grandparents. I've lived with my biological parents all my life. I call my two grandparents 'parents' because I still see them and I have been calling them grandma and grandpa all my life."

Kecia told us that although she really has only two parents, she sometimes considers her aunt to be a parent too. She said, "My two parents are my mom and my dad. They're divorced. My 'third parent' is actually my aunt — my mom's brother's wife. She has been very nice to me and she has two kids, one of whom is my age. He and I used to have a lot of fun together when he went to my school. Anyway, my aunt acts like a mother to me sometimes. I like her a lot."

Sometimes it is hard to decide whether stepparents should be considered parents. Some of the kids in our class consider their stepparents to be almost like their biological parents and others consider them to be quite different. Caleb considers Heidi, his father's girlfriend, a third parent in some ways — after his father and his mother. He considers her a guardian parent of sorts, but he has never really thought of her as a substitute mother or substitute parent. He thinks that a parent is someone you want to live with and have as a guardian, whether they are your biological parent or not.

Another girl in our class has two stepparents, a stepmother and a stepfather, and she has a hard time deciding whether to consider them parents or not. They usually live separate from her, but they do take her to school, feed her, and care for her. It is confusing at times to decide whether or not these people should have the same authority and love that a parent has.

Kate doesn't think that children should always consider their biological parents to be their parents. She wrote, "If you were adopted and were brought up calling your adopted parents mommy and daddy, then one day you were told that you were adopted, that might not change the fact that you thought of these people as parents — at least in the long run it shouldn't. Even if these people didn't actually give birth to you, they love you perhaps more than your biological parents ever could."

Thus we realized that kids think about parents in different ways and we found out that some kids in our class have one, two, three, four, or five "parents." We think that it is important for each child to decide about parents for himself or herself because it might feel a little strange if this issue were left in confusion. To avoid confusion, we talk about "your parents" throughout the book, but we want you to apply the advice and discussions here to any adult you think of as your parent. And although we use our mothers or fathers as examples here, we hope that everyone reading this book will be able to "plug in" the people they consider to be their parents.

The Ideal Parent

We know that many parents wish that their children were perfect all the time — getting good grades, being talented and athletic, and acting mature and well behaved, even on special trips and vacations. Likewise, many of us sometimes wish we had perfect parents. While we know that this is impossible — that everyone has flaws and makes mistakes — we spent some time thinking about what the ideal parent would be like.

Elizabeth wrote, "Ideal parents would not be overprotective or spoiling. They would be very open with their children and would definitely be honest. They would not be strict but would not be loose. They would listen to their children's ideas and would be optimistic and encouraging. Rules about things concerning the children would be discussed and made in their presence. These parents would allow the children to disagree to some extent."

Mike wrote, "Ideal parents would spend lots of time with their kids but let the kids be alone if they wanted to be. They would let the kids do what they wanted to do as long as it wasn't something totally outrageous, like a five-year-old kid doing drugs. Ideal parents would trust kids to do some things, like set their own bedtime. They would not mind if the kids went to late parties or things like that. If they started staying out until 4 A.M. every night, the parents would sit them down and talk to them about it and make some rules that would help the kids stay out of trouble — while still having a good time."

Seth, a boy in our class, thinks that ideal parents should have a little bit of every parental quality, as well as being nice people. He wrote, "I think they would be helpful and kind and quite likable. I don't think they would have very many enemies but they would not be perfect. Ideal parents would be very patient and would rarely lose their temper. They would limit the nagging and the strictness but they wouldn't be too loose. They would be nice but they would stick to their rules, which would always be reasonable. They would be pleased by the happiness of others."

Macy thought about the kind of parent she would like to be when she is an adult. She wrote: "I always picture myself as the perfect mother when I grow up, with two perfect children and the perfect husband. Of course, this might not turn out to happen — I could end up with a drunkard husband and two drug-addicted kids. I keep preparing myself for that, but I can't help thinking about having two perfect kids.

"To be the ideal 'All-American Mom,' I think you need to be nice, but not let your children get away with murder. You should be interested in what your kids do, and spend a reasonable amount of time with them. You should still have time to do what you want without your kids too.

"The ideal mom would be open to discussion on any subject that is on the child's mind.

"I think that any kids fortunate enough to get ideal parents should treat them with the same kind of respect as they treat you."

As you can see from the opinions expressed above, we have many different thoughts about what makes a perfect parent. All of us generally agree with a few things. One boy in our class wrote, "An ideal parent is caring, loving, nice, understanding, and doesn't push you too much." We agree with these points. Kama wrote that her ideal parent would be "a person who could understand a kid's problems and maybe help with the problems. I think a parent should try to spend time with the child so they could get closer to each other." We agree with Kama's points. We also agree with Justin, who wrote: "I consider an ideal parent to be someone who cares about the child and isn't too loose but does have some restrictions. An ideal parent should not let the child have too much candy and should make sure the child eats vegetables. Also, an ideal parent shouldn't be too strict but should have rules, usually for the sake of the child."

Most parents are not ideal parents — in anyone's opinion — mainly because they are human. Some parents tend to be overprotective or worrying parents; others tend to be loose or careless. Some parents nag you a lot and others expect you to be perfect.

We talked a lot about different kinds of parents and we did some artwork and dramatic improvisations to show us exactly what we felt. We are aware that most parents do not fit into one category all the time, but we did want to think about the good and bad qualities of different kinds of parents and to make some suggestions about what to do if you have a certain kind of parent.

The Overprotective Parent

Overprotective parents are usually reluctant to let their children do things by themselves. They worry about your safety when crossing streets and hesitate to let you sleep over at other people's houses. They don't seem to want to let kids experience life on their own and they worry a whole lot and try to protect you from everything.

Overprotective parents make their children stick to strict bedtime rules (even on vacation), for fear that they will get sick. They won't let the children walk along a beach alone because they might fall into the water and drown, get eaten by big sharks and crabs, or fall into some quicksand and disappear forever. At an amusement park, overprotective parents won't let the children go on very scary rides because they might get hurt or throw up.

At mealtime, the overprotective parent urges you to eat all your vegetables and stay healthy. Sharp steak knives are not allowed because they might hurt you. At your birthday party, an overprotective parent wouldn't want you to eat too much cake (you might get sick!) and insists that you receive only gifts that are soft and are too large to swallow.

Watching television with overprotective parents can be an experience. They tell you not to sit too close to the television, for fear of hurting your eyes or receiving too much radiation. They limit the amount of television you can watch and they won't let you watch PG movies because they give kids "bad ideas."

Children of overprotective parents sometimes take dares from other kids because they know their parents wouldn't want them to. They also sometimes lie to their parents because they know they wouldn't approve of lots of the things that they do, and they lie to their friends because they feel silly telling other kids what their parents won't let them do.

What we like least about these parents is that they are not trusting and don't let kids learn on their own. You can't have much fun with overprotective parents and you can feel very childish. What we like most about these parents is that their children rarely get hurt and the kids seem healthier because they eat less junk food and sweets. If you have overprotective parents, you might also be glad that they think of you a lot and care about you, and when you need attention, you can get a lot of it.

Ana sometimes feels that her mother can be overprotective. When Ana's older sister was learning to drive a car, Ana wasn't allowed in the car with her and wasn't even allowed to walk along the same side of the street her sister was going to drive down. Ana thought her mom was a bit insecure about this matter and too overprotective.

If your parents are overprotective, you might try sitting down with them and talking to them about reasonable rules. You might talk to another adult (like a friend of your mother's) and ask the friend to help by speaking to your mother. You also might talk with your friends and find out what rules their parents have and give this information to your parents. Also, you could yell and scream at them a lot or try crying (they might feel sorry for you). If you have a father who won't let you cross a big street, you might show him that you can be responsible in little ways and then earn greater responsibilities.

The Spoiling Parent

Spoiling parents give kids too many things for no special reason. We find that they think their kids will be good if they are given lots of possessions. This amounts to bribery.

On a vacation, spoiling parents buy many gifts for their children. They also indulge them by letting them do all kinds of outrageous things. At bedtime they let the children watch television and don't care if they stay up late. If they really want them to go to bed, they promise to buy a gift the next day. At mealtime the kids of a spoiling parent get what they want to eat, not necessarily what they need.

You can tell the spoiling parents at a child's birthday party. They give the kid a lot of stuff, particularly the new fad gifts that are advertised on television. They also tend to reward their child with large allowances, special presents, and lots of fun trips.

What we like most about spoiling parents is obvious — they give us a lot of toys and, sometimes, a lot of attention. Also, the friends of these kids sometimes are given special treats too. What we like least about spoiling parents is that they do this too often, which is embarrassing, particularly if your allowance is a lot larger than that of all the other kids you know.

We know a boy named James who had two friends who recently received Atari cartridges. James complained to his mom that he didn't get one from her. His mother said that, unfortunately, these particular cartridges are too expensive, but instead she bought him a big and expensive box of baseball cards — all because his friends received some gifts!

Parents can use spoiling against each other if they are divorced. One girl in our class has divorced parents and she lives with her mother and her sister stays with her father. One day she went over to her dad's wearing a new pair of Nike sneakers bought by her mother. Her sister saw them and asked for a pair. The next time she went over to her dad's house, her sister had five pairs of Nikes!

Some kids like to be spoiled and others hate it. Still others feel mixed about it and seem able to recognize the good and bad aspects. For example, for nine years, Kate lived with her grandmother who Kate thinks "spoiled her rotten." Kate told us that it never embarrassed her and she never really minded it.

Some kids who have spoiling parents become selfish and greedy. They sometimes turn into spoiled brats and have little patience. They expect people to do exactly what they say and expect expensive presents from their friends. When they grow up they have problems because there is no one to give them what they want, like their parents did.

If you have spoiling parents and don't like it we have some suggestions. First of all, simply refuse to let them bribe you. Refuse their presents (even if they are tempting ones) and do not take advantage of them. This will require a lot of self-control. Also, set rules for yourself and your parents. You might also want to talk to them about it (over dinner at a nice restaurant) or find someone else who'll talk with them.

The Strict Parent

The strict parent is a parent who makes lots of rules and enforces them all the time. Many of these rules are inconvenient and are therefore easy to break. Even with this inconvenience, you may find that the strict parent punishes you more severely than the average parent would. The strict parent never lets a kid stay out late at night, and might tend to want to send the kid to a military academy or parochial school.

Strict parents set very early bedtimes that are strictly enforced. Quite simply, they allow no exceptions to their rules. At mealtime they are very proper (no elbows on the table!) and if you don't eat your vegetables, no dessert is permitted. Severe limitations are also imposed on television viewing — both the amount of time and the kinds of shows you are permitted to watch.

When strict parents punish kids, they take away their allowances for a month or ground them for a long period of time, whether the behavior being punished was a severe crime or returning home five minutes late. When strict parents reward you, they give a utilitarian reward — such as a watch (so you can be on time!). If you are very, very lucky, they will permit you to stay out half an hour later sometime.

We know that, in some cases, the parent is doing this all for the sake of the child and we think that the strict parent often has good intentions. What we like least about these parents is that, most of the time, they are strict for no reason at all that we can find, and their rules make no sense.

Fred, a boy we know, wanted to sleep over at John's house. He was really anxious about it and asked his parents for permission. His mother said that he couldn't because he had to do his schoolwork. Fred was a good student already, so this seems unreasonable. Besides, it was a weekend and there was plenty of time to do homework *and* sleep over at a friend's house.

Some kids raised by these kinds of parents may become wild if the parents are away because they need someone outside of them to impose any order or rules. Other kids may be very weird and different from their friends because they have to go to bed earlier than everyone else, for example.

If you believe your parents are too strict, we recommend that you sit down and talk to them. Give them some specific, factual examples of their strictness and ask them to be a little looser. It would also help if you show them that you can be pretty responsible on your own and don't need strict rules.

The Embarrassing Parent

The embarrassing parent regularly embarrasses you in front of your friends and relatives. Elizabeth has noticed that some parents do this subconsciously and others do it on purpose to punish their child. David thinks some parents use this as a threat to get their kids to behave and Kecia feels that some parents really don't try to break this bad habit and, if they did try, would find it hard to stop.

Embarrassing parents are easy to spot because of the awful situations that they put their kids into. For example, if you are sleeping over at a friend's house, this kind of parent will call you before bedtime to say "Have a nice time" and "Brush your teeth" and "I miss you." This could make you feel like a baby and could lead to an embarrassment. At your birthday party, with all your friends sitting around the table, an embarrassing parent would give you a present to open and it would be new underwear. The embarrassing parent is particularly tough to deal with when you have friends sleeping over. They might say to their twelve-year-old daughter in front of her friend, "Dear, it's time for *Sesame Street* — your *favorite* show!"

Elizabeth, who lives with her aunt, once had a friend overnight and they wanted to watch a PG movie. Her Aunt Sally said they were too young to watch it and Elizabeth felt childish. They got into an embarrassing argument and Elizabeth's friend felt very awkward.

Alan, a boy we know, has also felt embarrassed by arguments with his mom. Once they went to visit one of his mom's friends and she started talking about a fight they had recently had and began to tell all the reasons for the fight. Alan felt very uncomfortable and urged his mom not to do this again.

It is also very embarrassing to be playing in the street with a bunch of kids on a summer evening around 7:30 and have your parent call out to you "Dear, it's time to come in! Time for bed!"

There is almost nothing we like about embarrassing parents except that they usually aren't embarrassing all the time. What we like least about these parents is that they force their child into regular humiliations. We have noticed that children of embarrassing parents often seem self-conscious, defensive, and reluctant to say anything. Maybe they're afraid of getting humiliated in public.

We do have some suggestions about how to deal with this kind of parent. First you should try to ask your parent not to mention embarrassing things in front of your friends and relatives and not to humiliate you in front of other people. If that doesn't work, you should be sure to talk about the embarrassing things that they do as soon as they happen so they might not happen again. Finally, you might try to embarrass them in public so they know how it feels. This isn't the best thing to do, but it might have some effect on a bad situation.

The Loose Parent

Loose parents don't pay as much attention to their children as they should. They aren't as strict as many other parents and they aren't as protective. If you have loose parents, you may find that they don't come down on you as hard as other parents come down on their kids or as hard as they should.

Loose parents are easygoing about many things. They often let their kids stay up later than most people think is good for them. At mealtime, they don't care much about proper nutrition, and they usually don't make a big deal about not snacking before a meal. If you have a loose parent, you probably are not forced to eat what you don't want and you are probably allowed to stay up late watching any television shows you want. You're allowed to attend movies of any rating (including X-rated films) and you probably get to see some very scary movies.

The loose parent punishes a child only if the child is very, very bad and then lets the child decide what kind of punishment is appropriate. Loose parents reward their kids by buying expensive gifts. Kids of loose parents are often spoiled.

One kid we know has a father who is very loose. One time the kid went to the refrigerator and took out a beer and started to drink it and the father didn't even mind. This kid is only thirteen. He doesn't have a bedtime and can usually stay up as late as he likes.

Macy has a friend who tells a similar story. Her friend was sleeping over at another friend's house when the friend's mother came into the room and said, "Anybody want a beer?" The kid thought it was a joke and said "Yes," and a few minutes later, the mother came back with two pitchers of beer. These kids were eleven and thirteen and felt obligated to take a sip of the beer, even though they weren't really interested. While this might seem to be a funny story, most of us think that this mother was irresponsible and should not have given beer to these kids. Some of us don't think this is such an awful crime, but we still think the parent was probably too loose.

What we like most about loose parents, or any parent when she or he acts like a loose parent, is that they don't bother us about bedtime or house rules. It's easy to take advantage of them and get what you want. Also, having a loose parent can make you very responsible and very independent because you have to set the rules for yourself. What we like least about these parents is that they are not as concerned about their child as they should be and the child may feel that the parents don't care. Some kids with loose parents feel that other things (like work, friends, or hobbies) are more important to them than their kids. Some loose parents are actually guilty of child neglect and making their kids act like fully grown adults.

We have noticed that kids with loose parents are often upset when they have to follow certain rules. For instance, if they sleep over at someone else's house and have to go to bed at a certain time, they don't like it and are not very cooperative. Some kids with loose parents act quite spoiled and brag a lot about their situation and may tend to act out a lot in school.

If you have a loose parent and are concerned about it, we suggest you ask your parent to make at least a few reasonable rules (like about using machines or tools that are very dangerous). You might want to explain that it is fun to have a lot of independence, but things can get ridiculous if the parent doesn't take some responsibility.

The Nagging Parent

The nagging parent yells at us a lot. He or she spends a lot of time repeatedly telling us to clean our rooms, that we're watching too much television, eating too fast, eating with our mouths open, eating the wrong foods, forgetting to do our chores, and not working on our homework. The nagging parent can get these messages to us in many ways: yelling at us, dropping obnoxious little hints, lecturing us.

Nagging parents are at their worst at mealtime and at bedtime. At bedtime, nagging parents remind us that it is time to go to bed, even if we remember on our own. We are told to be in bed on time, brush our teeth, be in bed on time, brush our teeth, be in bed on time . . . At mealtime, we are told to eat our vegetables, drink plenty of milk, cut out the Twinkies, stop poking at our food, even eat Brussels sprouts! Some nagging parents urge their kids not to eat too fast (or slow) and to be sure to eat a lot because they might starve (or eat less because they might get too fat).

At a birthday party, it is easy to spot a nagging parent. This is the parent who reminds you to take care of your new toys and, after you open a present, says "Now say thank you, Jeffrey." A nagging parent guilt-trips you by reminding you many times to say thank you. "These nice people took the bother to come all the way across town, just to do something nice for you." A nagging parent would also nag the child having the birthday party about cleaning up after the party and probably expect the kid's friends to clean up also. We find that nagging parents rarely actually end up imposing punishment on their children. Instead they nag them with threats about punishment a whole lot, but they rarely carry the threats out.

What we like most about nagging parents is that they are trying to get the kid to do what they think is right, so there are good intentions involved. What we like least about nagging parents is that they tend to nag and yell too much.

A girl in our class once slept over at a friend's house so that the two girls could do homework together. While they were in the friend's room, working hard on their homework, the friend's mother came in to remind them to do their homework, even though they were already doing it. She reminded them several times about the homework, and after she stopped nagging about the homework, she started talking about taking out the trash. After that, she was reminding her daughter to clean the kitty litter box. As it turned out, the girls never had a chance to finish their homework — all due to the nagging mother.

Children who have nagging parents sometimes appear to be withdrawn or spaced out. They sometimes have trouble listening well and can be irresponsible when there isn't anyone around to nag them a lot. On the other hand, we have noticed some cases where the child may develop good habits because of the constant reminders sent their way.

If you have parents who nag too much, we urge you to talk to them about it. If they are under a great deal of stress, due to something such as divorce, loss of job, or the death of a close friend or relative, try to be patient and understand that the nagging might be temporary. Another suggestion is to nag them back. Then they might realize how it feels to be the target of such nagging.

The Parent with Great Expectations

Some parents expect more from us than we can reasonably accomplish. We call this a "parent with great expectations." These parents expect their children to do everything perfectly in every area: schoolwork, sports, arts, music, popularity. They also expect them to do more than their share of chores. Sometimes, parents who were superb athletes as kids expect their children to be the same way and push them as if they were also superb athletes. Mindy thinks that such parents may be motivated by the desire for their children to have a better life than they did, so they don't often look at the kinds of pressures they place on their kids.

The parent with great expectations expects the child to study, even while on vacation, which is meant to be fun. If you are camping, you are expected to start a fire with no matches. If you are at the beach, they expect you to swim long distances. If you go to a fancy hotel, they may ask you to play the piano in front of total strangers. Generally, you will find yourself guilt-tripped into being very responsible and careful during the whole vacation.

At mealtime, you are expected to have really good manners, and keep up your part of an "interesting" discussion. You are expected to eat at the perfect speed and to tolerate (or even like) strange and disgusting food like squid, snails, spinach, and broccoli. At your birthday party, you are expected to have a lot of friends to invite and to behave perfectly the whole time. You might be expected to take your friends to see some sophisticated ballet rather than to a video game arcade. The parent with great expectations expects you to open the birthday card before the present and not to be greedy at all. You have to send thank you notes right after the party and be very courteous and grateful to the people who gave you gifts. You are also expected not to complain about such things as having to wear a scratchy new sweater.

When this kind of parent punishes you, you are actually expected to confess to the crime and say something like

"I've been bad. I deserve punishment." You are also expected to accept the punishment and not try to find a way to get out of it. When it comes to television rules, the parent generally expects the child to want to read or do homework. Television viewing may be limited to news shows or educational shows. This kind of parent makes you watch *Nova* and expects you to present a full report on the show before you go to bed.

What we like most about parents with great expectations is that they present us with great challenges. With a parent like this, a kid could find himself or herself getting very good at some things. What we like least about these parents is that they push too much. They talk about you growing up to be a doctor or a lawyer and they make you feel as if you have disappointed them if you do anything different than what they expect. The pressure is very great with this kind of parent around.

Some of us have parents with great expectations and some of us know parents of other kids who are like this. Elizabeth has a friend who does well in school and her mother expects her to get straight A's. When the friend came home with a report card of all A's and one B, she ended up crying and feeling badly. Kecia has a friend who is very pretty; she is five-one and weighs ninety pounds. This girl's mother always criticizes her appearance or says things like "Stop eating! You're too fat!"

We know other parents who are generally not this kind of parent but who sometimes have greater expectations than we'd like. Caleb sometimes shows his mother a drawing he has worked on for a long time and his mother says, "It's good but it's not your best." Caleb feels he doesn't need this kind of feedback. Jasanne usually finds that she wakes up on time for school either because her mother wakes her or because she sets her own alarm. One day she didn't set her alarm and her mother didn't wake her and then her mother got angry and upset and blamed her for getting to school late. Jasanne didn't think this was fair.

Some kids with parents with great expectations are very competitive and are perfectionists. Sometimes they can be quite conceited. At other times they are insecure and put themselves down and are very self-conscious.

If you have a parent with great expectations, or if your parents sometimes expect too much from you, we think you should talk to them about the pressures they are making you feel. You might want to give some thought to looking at what their parents were like to them and trying to understand why your parent is acting this way. You also might find that you like them having great expectations of you and that you study harder and work harder to meet their goals.

Recognizing Your Parents' Flaws

We think that most kids will recognize a little bit of each of these kinds of parent in their own mother or father. Our parents tend to act differently at different times — sometimes nagging, sometimes overprotective, sometimes loose, sometimes with great expectations. Part of the difficulty in dealing with parents is that you can't always tell what mood they'll be in or when they'll act like one of these kinds of parents. Sometimes you'll mention something to them, expecting them to react as overprotective parents ("No, you may not go to the rock concert next week!"), and, instead, they'll respond like loose parents ("That sounds like fun. Can I drive you and your friends to the concert?"). We haven't found a sure way to tell which mood a parent will be in at any particular time but we have found that, after living with parents for a few years, you get some sense of when they're in different moods or you notice different clues that let you know what condition they're in.

Every parent has some small things that they do that kids think are wrong and that drive us crazy. These are called flaws. It's important to learn to recognize your parents' flaws and to develop a realistic attitude toward them. Some flaws that parents have can be corrected with a little bit of help from kids, along with the will to change from the parents. Some flaws cannot be changed. A flaw that can't be changed is part of your parent's personality and, as long as it is only a flaw, we recommend that you get used to it. You're going to have to live with it for a while.

Here are some of the flaws that we've noted in our parents:

being impatient
yelling too easily
being a health nut
embarrassing you in public
having a closed mind
changing their minds a lot
being obnoxious in public
nagging
using old-fashioned words
being a bad cook
forgetting birthdays
acting too sweet
talking loudly
pretending to listen to you
letting people push them around
picking fights over nothing
making arrangements with kids and then breaking them
being stubborn
driving too slowly
never being home
being lazy

When we get into a situation where we have to deal with our parents' flaws, we try to decide which flaws we can really influence and which are hopeless. Sometimes it's helpful to stick up for yourself and other times that will just make matters worse. Kate told us, "My mother insists that there is a certain way to eat communion wafers and I say that there isn't and that I don't like to eat them her way. So, whenever there's communion, I eat the wafer my way. Then she glares at me, but she gets the message that I am not going to eat it her way."

Macy has not done anything to influence her parents' flaws. She told us, "I have never dealt with any of my parents' flaws because I don't think they will change, and that's part of their charm."

When parents criticize you for something that is also a weakness of theirs, it's helpful to point this out. Joachim said, "My mother yells at me for leaving my bedroom light on, but she also does that, so I tell her that she does it too. This makes her stop complaining for a while."

We don't expect our parents to be perfect. We do expect them to be open to criticism and suggestions from us and we want them to try not to be so defensive when we have a gripe or complaint. It seems clear to us that the best relationships kids can have with parents involve open talking between the parent and the child. This can help you work through any problems that come up and can show you that your opinion is worth the adult's consideration. This is particularly helpful when we talk about certain key issues upon which kids and parents often disagree.

PART II

Resolving Differences with Your Parents

Fighting

At some time or other, all kids have fights with their parents. If you think about it, you might realize that you and your parents disagree on things all the time. Sometimes these problems get solved quickly and without a big deal; other times, these disagreements turn into major fights and become important issues between parents and kids. It is important to think about the ways in which we resolve these disagreements. Through talking with our classmates about how we deal with problems at home, we've learned new techniques for dealing with our parents. We've also learned that both the parent and the child have to take responsibility for finding good ways to disagree and still continue living together. No one wants to fight all the time.

We don't think there's anything wrong with fighting. It's perfectly normal for two people to disagree about something and for each to want to convince the other person that his or her point of view is the best. We've seen lots of cases, however, of parents and kids fighting in ways that are just not fair or healthy. We think it's important for people to think about what ways of fighting are okay and what ways are not okay.

Parents sometimes over-react when they disagree with a kid about something. We don't like it when parents yell or get violent and hit kids. We also think it's unfair for parents to issue extreme punishments like grounding a kid just because of a simple disagreement. Other parents sometimes guilt-trip their kids heavily and we think this isn't a good thing to do either. Some of us think that the worst thing a parent can do is not to forgive a kid after a fight. This can cause a lot of long-term problems in a family.

Kids also fight in some ways that we don't think are really fair or helpful. Throwing a temper tantrum and swearing at a parent is not a helpful way to disagree. Some kids yell and run into their room and slam the door. We know some kids who take out their anger on someone who had nothing to do with the fight — particularly a younger brother or sister. This just isn't fair at all. And as much as it sounds appealing to us at times, running away from home isn't really a solution to problems you have with your parents either. You need to find a better way to work out the difficulties.

We've noticed three different kinds of fighting that go on between parent and child: physically violent fighting, verbal fighting, and "the silent treatment."

Physical fighting involves hitting, punching, and slapping and is not at all a good way for a family, or anyone, to work out problems. One problem with this is that the parent is usually a lot bigger and stronger than the kid and this difference in strength can be used unfairly against the child. We've also heard of cases of teenagers beating up their parents. We don't recommend this either.

Verbal fighting involves arguing, yelling, insulting, swearing, talking loudly, and waving your hands and fingers. This can be a scary way to fight also, and can leave kids feeling frightened and upset if it's not kept under control. Most of us think this is a lot better than physical fighting, but it can be hurtful too.

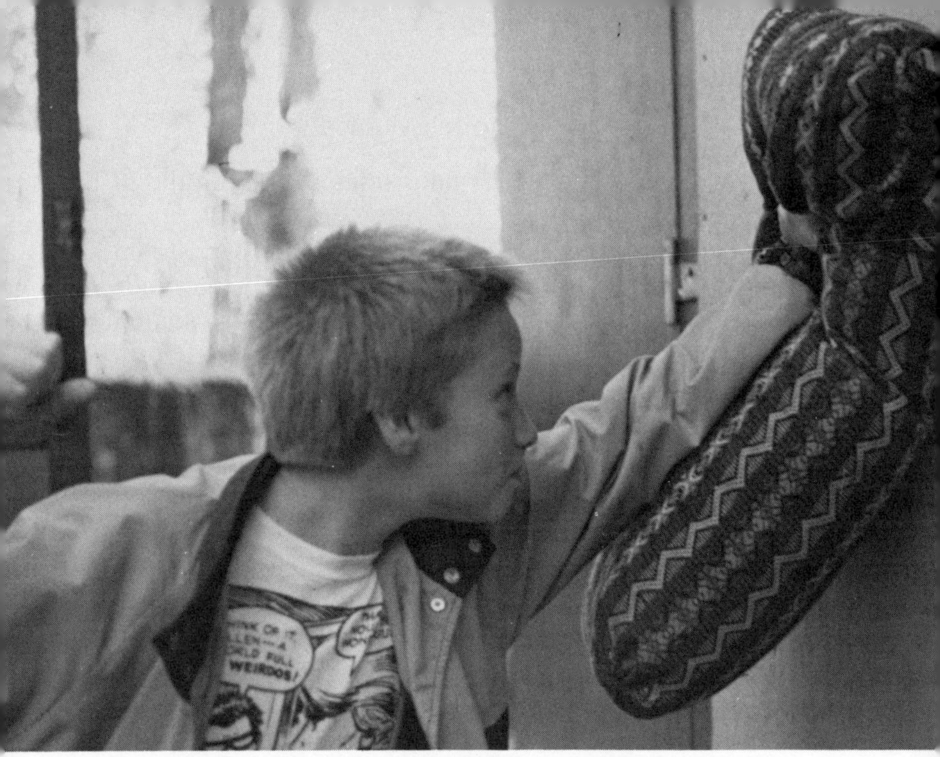

Punching a pillow when you're angry can be helpful.

"The silent treatment" is when people fight without words and just go around ignoring each other and avoiding any eye contact. Some of us also call this kind of fighting "cold war," because people don't interact except when absolutely necessary and act very cold and distant to one another. This can last for a few minutes or for many days. It doesn't resolve the problem that is causing the tension.

As much as we realize that fighting occurs in every family, we think that some ways of disagreeing and working through conflict are better than others. Sitting down and calmly talking about a disagreement is often very helpful. Both the parent and the child, however, need to talk *and* listen. People should try to understand the other side of the situation and compromise when necessary. It's also sometimes helpful to bring someone else in to help you clear up the situation, but this has to be a neutral party and someone who won't take sides in the middle of the disagreement.

When things get really hot and kids and parents start to fight, we recommend that you split up and go and cool off. Talking to a friend can be helpful, because sometimes you just have to get bad feelings off your chest and then things will be okay. Going into separate rooms and punching pillows can be helpful too.

Sometimes people fight about things that really aren't even worth fighting about. We've noticed that this happens when the parent or the kid has something stressful going on in their lives. This once happened to Kecia. She got into a fight with her mother about not putting the cap on the toothpaste tube. Kecia's mom yelled at her for not putting the cap back on the tube and then Kecia reminded her mother that she had left her ashtray in Kecia's room. Kecia then picked up the ashtray and threw it into the trash can. This seems like a big deal to make about an ashtray and the cap of a toothpaste tube, but what was really happening was that her mother had a tough day at her job and Kecia had gotten a pretty bad grade on a test. They were taking out their problems on one another.

Some people just argue for the sake of arguing. One boy we know, Allen, got into a verbal fight with his mother about where he came from. Allen insisted that he came from God and his mother disagreed and told him he was wrong. It was clear to both of them that they didn't really care about the answer but were arguing for the pure sake of arguing. Jonathan had one of these fights with his mother: They argued about whether or not the English language was going to stop being spoken in the near future!

Macy told us about a fight with her parents that made her feel guilty: "A few weeks ago, I lost my Thermos and told my mother I had left it in my father's car. When we discovered that I had not, my mother and father got angry at me 'cause I was so forgetful. About three days later, it was Valentine's Day and my mother got me a new Thermos for a present, which made me feel happy and foolish at the same time. Around three weeks later, I found my moldy lunch and original Thermos. I threw out my lunch and the old Thermos and felt very guilty about it."

Problems can come up when kids get involved in fights between their parents. If your parents are fighting, we suggest you don't interfere, but simply leave the room. Later, after things have calmed down, you might want to go in and comfort your parents, but it really isn't a good idea to get too involved in the actual fight. It's a good idea not to bother them with little things after they've been fighting and to try to be good about your chores and responsibilities.

One time, Gillian's parents were having a big fight, throwing things around and yelling. Gillian and her sister went into their room to keep out of the fight. Afterward, Gillian sat down with her mother at the table and tried to comfort her because she was still upset. That helped her mother and made both of them feel a lot better.

Humor can be very helpful in fights between parents and kids. Macy told us, "Once I was starting to get into a fight with my mother and I told her to stop the fighting. I told her that anytime we started to fight again, we should both say the word *food*. This helped for a while."

Macy also told us about a particularly angry fight she was having with her mother. "I started insulting her," Macy said. "But she didn't get angry and act the way I expected her to act. Instead she cracked up and, for some reason, found me to be comical. This was not how I had wanted it to be, but it made me feel better anyway."

Ana once stayed at a friend's house half an hour later than she was supposed to. When Ana's mother became worried, she called the police, who found Ana and brought her home. Ana's mother yelled at her and asked her why she hadn't called to say that she'd be late. Ana answered by saying that she didn't know the telephone number. So her mother wrote the number on Ana's stomach.

If both the parent and the child are calm, they can discuss a disagreement or a difficult issue without fighting and sometimes reach a very satisfactory conclusion. When Kecia was eleven, she felt that her mother was being very overprotective because Kecia wasn't allowed to do a lot of the things her friends could do. They sat down together and talked about it. Her mother hadn't known that Kecia felt this way and, together, they were able to work out a compromise.

Again, no matter what the problem, the important thing is the way in which parent and child work it out. Because some parents and kids spend so much of their time fighting in harmful ways, some families don't have a lot of good feelings between child and parent. All kids and parents should think about the best ways for their family to work through their problems and to try to find a way that works and doesn't upset too many people.

Allowances

An allowance is an amount of money that someone (usually a kid) receives on a weekly or monthly basis. Children usually receive allowances from their parents and may be expected to use the money on a wide range of things, including video games, records, movies, presents for relatives and friends, dates, bicycle parts, and tickets to concerts or sporting events.

Parents and children have disagreements about allowances usually because children want more money than the parent can or wants to give the child. Kids and parents seem to have an almost infinite number of excuses for getting or giving more or less allowance. This tends to be the subject of an ongoing debate.

We have different thoughts about what a child should be expected to pay for out of an allowance. A lot of this depends on how much the allowance is and what items a child wants and needs. Caleb said that what a child should pay for depends on the kind of family involved: "The kids should be expected to buy the things that they want, but might get help from the parent if the object is really expensive. In other cases, the child might be expected to buy stuff that they need, like clothing and food, not just the things that they want."

Jesse feels that kids should be expected to pay for "movies, video games, toys, hobbies, etc." Tanya feels that it is best to get a smaller allowance and only pay for extras "such as toys, candy . . . and the parent should pay for the necessary items like lunch, clothing."

Even among the kids in our class there is a lot of disagreement about how much allowance kids should get at certain ages. Gillian feels that a six-year-old should get up to $1 a week, a nine-year-old should get from $1.50 to $2, a twelve-year-old should get $3 to $4. Mike thought the six-year-old should get about $1, the nine-year-old should get $2.50, the twelve-year-old should get $3.50, and a fifteen-year-old should get between $15 and $20 if expected to pay for clothing and other major items. John feels that the amount of allowance really depends on the individual

Kids spend their allowances on all kinds of things.

child and his or her needs — not on age alone.

We think that parents have the final decision on what a child's allowance will be — mainly because the parent is the one who pays the allowance. However, we think that the parent and the child should sit down together and look at the factors that are involved in what the child wants and needs. For example, Mike thinks that they should look at "the child's social life and the amount of relatives the kid has to buy presents for." Jesse thinks that you should "sit down and make a list of the things you need to buy. Add a little extra for odds and ends and you'll have what you need." In general, we agree with Caleb who thinks "it should be decided both with the child's age in mind and what both the kid and the parent think is a reasonable amount of money."

Some parents make their kids do chores or housework in order to earn their allowance. We think that the two issues should be usually kept separate. Kids should take on their share of responsibilities around the house, whether or not they get paid for it, and they should get some kind of allowance, whether or not they have household jobs to do. In some cases, however, parents tie the allowance to the chores because, if they didn't, the kid would never do the chores.

Different kids in our class get different amounts of allowances and are expected to buy different things with the money. Some of us feel good about our allowances and others don't. David told us, "At the moment, I get $1.50 each week. I started to get an allowance when I was six years old and I got 25¢ then. I like getting an allowance, but I wish it were higher."

Kama told us, "I get $5 each week. When I was around eight or nine years old, I got $10, but I had to pay for a lot of things out of that. Now my grandmother sends me $5 each week, and in the summer, I get more for working in her store. I like my allowance, but I wish it were higher."

Gillian doesn't get an allowance anymore. She said, "My parents used to give me a dollar each week. When I started to baby-sit, they didn't give me the dollar anymore. They gave me good reasons for this and I agreed with them."

If the purpose of the allowance is to allow kids to buy some of the things they want or need, it makes sense to take the allowance away when they are old enough to work and make enough money to pay for their own needs. Some kids don't like their allowance to end, however.

If kids don't get any allowance, or want a bigger allowance, they should sit down and talk to their parents. They should present their point of view, listen to their parents' point of view, and come to a decision together, if at all possible. John suggests this method of determining the allowance: "The kid should make an offer and then the parent should make a counteroffer. They should both consider whether or not the kid has a job outside the home and also the kid's expenses."

Jesse found out that talking to his dad about an allowance was helpful. He told us, "For a long time, I hadn't been getting an allowance and a few of my friends were getting an equipment allowance — this is money on a monthly basis that pays for bicycle parts. So I asked my father for one. Since I hadn't been getting anything at all, it sounded reasonable to him and so we sat down and talked about it. We decided upon the figure of $50 for every three months. So far it's worked out really well."

Sometimes you'll find that parents will surprise you with their generosity, even when you think they might give you a hard time about it. Caleb said, "Recently, I asked my father if I could have a raise in my allowance, which had been at about $1 for the past three years. Sometimes it's pretty hard to talk to my father about things like this, and I was all ready to compromise at around $3, but I was surprised when he offered $5. Afterward — although I definitely liked the raise I got — I felt a little guilty because of the size of the allowance."

Some kids can be given allowances that are too big and this isn't good for them. This usually comes from parents who like to spoil their kids or parents who just don't care. This could cause problems because the kid probably wouldn't know what to do with a lot of money and might spend it without thinking. Caleb said, "If a child is going to get an allowance, the parent should make sure that it's the right amount of money and that the kid knows how to spend it."

Mike thinks that "if children get an allowance that is too big, they could get spoiled or could start thinking that they are better than other kids, just because of their bigger allowance."

Some parents stop allowance payments as a punishment. We don't think this is fair, except if the child's allowance is based on chores and the chores don't get done. Little kids need their money for certain things and they don't have another way to get money. As John put it, "If parents say they're going to give their kids x dollars a week, they should give them x dollars each week." This is an agreement that shouldn't be broken. There are other ways to punish a child and not break this agreement.

Baby-sitting

Baby-sitting becomes an issue between kids and parents when kids feel they're too old for a baby-sitter, or older siblings are forced to baby-sit for younger siblings, or your parents hire a baby-sitter you don't like.

Kate once had a baby-sitter who told her a lot of gory stories about people being murdered and raped and kidnaped. Kate became so scared that she couldn't get to sleep until a long time after her parents returned home. Kate told her parents about it and they never used this baby-sitter again.

Jake has a friend who got into a fight with his baby-sitter, and the baby-sitter walked out. When the parents came home, they were not very happy.

Mindy told us, "Once, a baby-sitter was watching a

friend and me and we were bad. The baby-sitter locked us in a room. When my mom came home, I told her, and I never had this baby-sitter again."

We think it is important for parents to hire good baby-sitters for kids. We want baby-sitters who are patient, responsible, resourceful, reasonably mellow, and attentive. Jasanne thinks baby-sitters should be concerned about safety and should have good manners and a businesslike attitude. Jake thinks that good baby-sitters shouldn't yell and certainly should never hit the child.

We feel different ways about whether or not older brothers and sisters should be expected to baby-sit for their siblings. Josh has found himself in this situation, and he thinks that older siblings could often be expected to baby-sit but should have some say in the matter. Josh said, "If they really don't want to do it, I don't think they should, unless the family has some special arrangement about it. The family could compromise and the older brother or sister could baby-sit only when nothing special is happening or maybe only half the times they are needed. I think that they should get paid. After all, they are working extra and maybe even missing special activities."

Caleb thinks this should depend on the family. He said, "The parents shouldn't force the older child to baby-sit for the younger one, but if it is something that the family agrees on, and the child isn't going to miss out on something he or she wanted to do, then this kind of baby-sitting can be an easy way to take care of the younger child. On the other hand, if the job is a drag and the older child is going to miss out on something, then payment sounds like a good idea."

If the siblings involved do not normally get along, or the older sibling always picks on the younger one, the parent should be careful about putting them into a baby-sitting situation. This could leave the younger kid open to a bad experience.

Once you get to be nine, ten, eleven, or twelve, you might feel you don't need or want a baby-sitter anymore. In general, we think children are ready to go without baby-sitters when they are old enough to be responsible for themselves, know what to do in an emergency situation, and feel comfortable alone. This will vary in age from child to child.

Josh suggests a way to test out if a child is ready to go without a baby-sitter. He said, "A family could leave the kid alone for half an hour, just as a test, and if the kid is okay, extend it. Keep doing this until both the parents and the child are confident about the child staying alone in the house."

It can be fun to baby-sit for a baby sister or brother.

Many of us have had experiences with being embarrassed because some of our friends had stopped having baby-sitters and we still had them — even, sometimes, when we felt we didn't need them and our parents insisted on keeping one. Nate told us, "I was asked to sleep over at someone's house and I was not able to because my mom already asked a baby-sitter to sit for me that night. When I told my friend why I could not sleep over, he started teasing me about still having a baby-sitter."

Sometimes the embarrassment is worth it. Kate told us, "When I was ten, I had a baby-sitter and, when I got to be almost eleven, I got kind of embarrassed about it, but I was really afraid to be alone in the house. So I decided that I'd rather be a little embarrassed than terrified."

Parents can help their children with this by not telling a lot of people about their baby-sitter if the kid tells them not to. Also, parents should listen carefully to kids' concerns about an age to stop the baby-sitter. Another good thing that we've heard about is, if there are a few kids in the family and the oldest kid is eleven or so and doesn't want a baby-sitter anymore, the parent can, in fact, hire the baby-sitter for the younger siblings and make it clear that the older kid has to take care of him- or herself. This takes care of the younger kids' need for care and the older kid's need for independence.

Bedtimes

Bedtime seems to be an issue between kids and parents because parents care about their children's health and don't want them to be tired, and children feel that they can judge for themselves what is best. Jonathan thinks,

"Most kids would like to stay up as long as they can, but parents find this bad for kids and would also like to have some quiet time in the house after the kids are in bed." We agree with Jesse, that, for many children, "it doesn't really matter when they go to bed, but they see this as a sort of game they play to see how far their parents will go."

Both parents and children should have a role in deciding when bedtime should be. The parents' duty is to see that the children get enough sleep so that they're not grumpy, tired, or short on patience on the next day, and to make sure the children have the time to have fun and do what they want to do in the evening. As Mike said, "The parent's role is to make the bedtime early enough to keep the child from being exhausted the next day and late enough to keep the kid happy."

The child's role in this decision is to talk to the parent about what the bedtime should be and try to come up with an agreement that both can live with. Children could gather information from their friends, so they know whether their bedtime is the same or very different from that of other kids their age.

Jesse talked about what he sees are reasonable bedtimes for kids at certain ages: "I feel that there should be some standard bedtimes for children. At six years old, I'd say it's around 7:30 because smaller kids get grouchy easily. At nine years old, around 8:30, because they get to stay up late enough to watch a prime time television show, and still get enough sleep. At twelve years old, bedtime could range from 9:00 to 11:00, and some kids should be able to decide when they are going to bed, depending on how tired they are. After about fourteen years old, any time would be fine, as long as the kid can focus on schoolwork the next day."

We think it's important for most kids to have set bedtimes because we've found that sometimes, if you stay up very late, you get tired the next day and regret it. Justin told us, "When I sleep over at my friend's house, he goes to bed whenever he wants. We usually stay up really late. The next day, I feel very tired and irritable. I think it's better with some limit."

If you want your bedtime changed, we think it's perfectly reasonable to sit down with your parents and tell them all the reasons it should be changed. Parents should listen with an open mind and consider making the change. Josh told us about how this happened in his family: "During my fourth grade year, I thought that 8:00 lights out was too early. I told my mom, and after she thought about it a while, she thought that I was right. From then until about sixth grade, I had to be in my room by 9:00, but I could stay up later if I was quiet."

Mike had a similar experience: "My mom and I once got into a big fight about bedtime. She wanted me to go to bed at what I thought was an excessively early time (9:30, or something like that) and I didn't want to. We sat down and talked about it and finally agreed on a later bedtime."

Heather told us about an experience she had with a friend that helped get her bedtime changed: "Last year, I spent the night at a person's house. She was eleven, and at 7:30, her mother came in and said, 'Time for bed girls!' It was pretty unreasonable. The next morning, we were eating breakfast and my friend asked me what time my bedtime was. I told her 9:30. This was in front of her mother. About a week later, her bedtime was two hours later. I feel that my friend did the right thing by talking to me in front of her mother, because it probably helped her mother to see what time would be a more suitable bedtime."

Once a bedtime is changed, it's sometimes hard for parents to get us to go to bed at that time. They don't realize that you might be in the middle of an important television show, or that you might not really be tired. It's important to be ready with a good excuse when you want to stay up later. Here's a list of excuses we've used:

"This is my favorite television show."
"I'm not tired."
"I'm old enough to decide myself."
"I want to read."
"I have homework to do."
"There's a really good movie on tonight."
"I went to bed early last night."
"It's been scientifically proven that a person can live a healthy, productive life on only fifteen minutes of sleep."
"I always go to bed on time. Make this night a special treat."
"Oh, just a little longer . . ."
"John gets to stay up as late as he wants."
"I need to get a drink of water and go to the bathroom."
"I have to set out my clothes for tomorrow."
"I only have two hundred more baseball cards to sort."
"I'm expecting an important phone call."
"The cat has to be let out."
"I have to watch this TV show for my social studies class."

But you should be prepared for your parents to give you one of these answers:

"You'll be grouchy in the morning, I know you."
"You have a busy day ahead of you."
"I let you stay up later than most kids. The least you can do is go to bed when I ask you to."
"You'll have rings under your eyes tomorrow and look really bad."
"You won't be able to get up in the morning."
"Go to bed as a present to me."
"You stayed up late last night."
"Because I said so."
"I need some peace and quiet."
"The big game is tomorrow."
"You need your beauty sleep."

We know that parents mean well by trying to get us to go to bed at a reasonable hour, but sometimes we just don't want to and we wish parents would be more flexible.

We encourage all kids not to make a big deal about washing their face and brushing their teeth before they go to bed. Kids can get pretty dirty and grimy if they don't wash their faces every night, especially if they don't take regular showers and especially if they're getting to be teenagers. It feels good to brush your teeth before you go to sleep. As Jonathan put it, "It is gross to go to sleep with scum all over your face and teeth."

Chores

We think that except for very young children, every member of the family should be expected to do some kind of household chores. This teaches everyone to take care of the shared household space. We think it's not fair to expect just one or two people to care for the entire family space. Another good reason to have everyone doing chores, in Nate's opinion, is "so that everyone will be thought of as equals."

At different ages kids should have different expectations concerning chores. A thirteen-year-old can certainly take on more responsibility than a five-year-old. Everyone — regardless of age (except for very small children) — should be expected to take care of cleaning their own rooms and cleaning up after themselves. Also, if a child has pets, part of the responsibility should be taking care of the pet. Older children can make meals, set the table, and clean it up afterward (but not every night), and do more strenuous chores like taking out garbage cans, yard work, and heavy-duty cleaning. Younger kids can dust, pick up things, stack newspapers, and generally help with easy jobs.

Most of us agree with Kate, who said that "neither children nor adults should be paid to do simple household chores."

We made lists of the different chores we have to do. Here are some of them:

KAMA: wash dishes or load dishes in dishwasher, feed cats, take care of cats' litter box, pull down shades, set table

JAKE: feed my lizard, do the laundry, make my bed, clean my room, take out the garbage

STEPHEN: set the table every other day, keep my room straightened up, do other odd jobs

HEATHER: clean the cat box and feed the cat, sometimes help with dinner, set and clear the table, clean my room, sometimes vacuum the living room, wash the dishes

NATE: clean room, clean bathroom, cook dinner, do dishes, walk the dog, rake the backyard

Most of us were assigned these chores and, while we might have had a chance to talk about them, it was clear that these were our expected jobs. Nate told us how his family decided on chores: "My family and I sat down and discussed who would do what jobs. After the talk, we all agreed upon our jobs." This sounds fair and reasonable for families to do.

While it is certainly reasonable for kids to be expected to keep their rooms neat enough, clean up after themselves, and make their beds, there are jobs that some of us think kids shouldn't be expected to do on a regular basis: Heather thinks that "washing the windows and keeping other people's rooms clean" are not reasonable jobs. Kate thinks that expecting a child to clean the whole house is also not fair and Stephen thinks that making dinner every night and doing all the gardening are too much for kids to do.

All of us use excuses, at times, to avoid doing our chores or doing other tasks that we are asked to do. For fun, we made a list of all the excuses we could think of that we have used:

"I feel sick."
"I'm doing my homework."
"My favorite show is on."
"I'll do it tomorrow."
"Get Marty [a sibling] to do it."
"Wait until a commercial."
"I have a headache."
"I have to wash my hair."
"I have to go over to a friend's house."
"I'm playing a game."
"I'm on the phone."
"It will mess up my clothes."
"It's my birthday."
"It's my room and I like it messy."
"I was just leaving."

We recommend that kids change their excuses from day to day. If you use the same excuse all the time, your parent

Everyone in the family should be expected to do household chores.

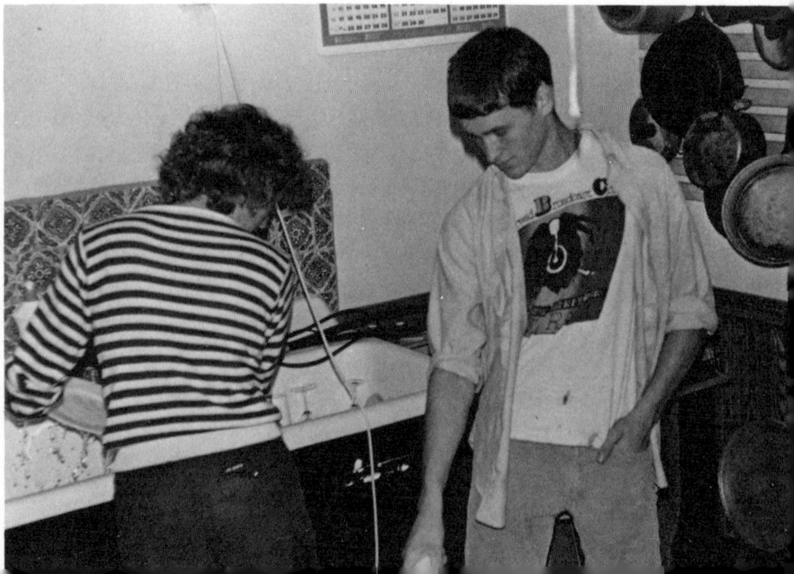

doesn't believe it or else just gets real angry. Also, you should be sure to sound sincere when you use an excuse and pretend that you really mean it. Sometimes this will work and other times your parent will force you to do the chore anyway.

We also made a list of things our parents say to us to get us to do chores, even after we make an excuse explaining why we shouldn't. It's important for kids to be aware of the strategies parents use, because sometimes you can think of good answers that make them leave you alone for a while. Some of the things our parents have said to us to get us to do chores (and in answer to our excuses) are:

"You're going to forget."
"You said that before."
"We're going to be eating then."
"I don't believe you."
"You're getting paid for this."
"You have enough responsibility to do it now."
"Do it for your mother."
"You don't do enough work around here."
"Do it for me."
"I'll tell your father (or mother)."

Stephen told us that his parents have used different strategies to get him to do his chores. He said, "They have used logic, threats, and anger." Sometimes these things work and sometimes they don't.

What punishments are used against us to get us to do the chores? David's parents have responded with more chores, no television, no friends over, no phone calls, and no going outside. Nate's mom has said he can't stay out late and that he will get no allowance. Other kids get yelled at, guilt-tripped, grounded, and have smaller privileges taken away. In general, we think it's a good idea for all kids to be given a reasonable amount of chores and to find a way to get them done without too much grief for either the kid or the parent.

Clothing

Clothing should not be a big deal between parents and kids. For very young kids, it usually isn't, because they don't really care what clothes they wear and haven't developed taste about what they like and don't like in fashion. But older kids, especially around ten, eleven, or twelve, start to care about clothes. They don't want to be humiliated by being forced to wear clothes that everyone thinks look stupid.

Parents need to have some say in the clothing that kids wear, mainly because they usually pay for it, and because they should make sure kids have warm enough clothes in the winter. While we admit that parents and kids won't always have the same tastes in clothes, it's important for parents to let kids choose their clothes, within reason. If the cost is too great or if the fashion is too repulsive to the parents, then they should say so. But if they just don't like the clothing, they shouldn't stop the child from buying it.

If your parent is pushing clothes on you that you don't want to wear, be as firm as you can and explain that you don't want them. Some parents want you to wear the kind of clothes they wish they could have worn as kids — even if you don't like them. And if you want some clothes that are not practical and your parents see no need for them, you should listen to them and be reasonable.

When Mike goes shopping with his mother, she gets very frustrated because he is so picky, so she just grabs anything off the rack and, if it fits, she buys it for him.

One time his mother saw this really tacky plaid coat and she asked Mike if he liked it. Instead of answering, he just walked away. His mother bought the coat, but he never wore it. Now it doesn't fit him anymore, but he wears it with his goggles and fins when he cleans his room.

Food

We understand that parents want us to eat good food so that we will grow up to be strong and healthy. We also know that they want to teach us good eating habits so that we don't get sick or hyperactive or weak and tired. We even understand that certain foods are good for us and certain foods aren't and we know that some of the things we eat could help to make us fat or depressed or sick.

This doesn't change the fact that some of our favorite foods are the exact foods that aren't good for us. Junk food

Kids tend to like junk food.

is a good example of the kind of foods we like even though we know it isn't very nutritionally good. Kate defines junk food as "chemically processed 'food' that is extremely bad for you, yet most people seem to be quite attached to it. Unfortunately, the things that are bad for you are often the things that taste good." She gives as examples of this kind of food, soda, candy, potato chips, corn chips, and fruit rolls.

Nate says that junk food is "food that is bad for your body but satisfying to your taste buds." His favorite junk foods are soda, Twinkies, gum, and candy.

We know that parents don't want us to eat these foods. Unfortunately, many of the foods they want us to eat are generally disgusting. We made a list of all the gross and disgusting foods we could think of that parents like kids to eat.

artichokes	kidney beans	salmon
beets	kiwi fruit	snails
broccoli	lamb	spinach
Brussels sprouts	lentil soup	squash
cabbage	lima beans	squid
cauliflower	liver	succotash
cheeses (certain ones)	mushrooms	tofu
clams	oatmeal	tongue
cow brains	pea soup	turnips
eggplant	poached eggs	yogurt
kale	quiche	zucchini

Not all of us find all of the above foods disgusting, but most of us do. We don't like it when our parents try to force us to eat some of these foods against our will and don't seem to understand that they are repulsive to us.

Jasanne told us, "I hate leafy green vegetables because they taste gross. My mother and I always argue about my not eating my greens. Two days ago, I had to answer some questions for school and one of them was to discuss a dietary issue between parent and child. My mother showed me a food chart, when she heard about this, and started reading: 'Leafy greens are a source of folic acid, vitamins A and C, calcium . . .' I said that I agreed with her and that what she told me was very educational. I still think leafy green vegetables are gross."

We think that our parents should know better than to try to force us into certain eating habits, because they were kids once too and they had the same problems with their parents. Kate told us a story that her mother told her: "When my mother was little, she refused to eat her succotash one night. My grandparents told her that she would have to sit at the table until she finished it. My mother said that she'd sit there until midnight, but she would not eat her succotash. So the table was cleared, except for her succotash, and the dishes were washed and my grandparents went into the living room to watch television. Still, my mother sat there. The succotash got very cold, but she still sat there and wouldn't eat it. After an hour or two, my grandparents decided it was a lost cause and sent my mother off to bed."

Parents tell you all kinds of things when they try to get you to eat some food that you don't want to go near. Some of the things our parents have said to try to convince us to eat are:

"It's good for you."
"You need your vitamins."
"This food will make you grow up to be strong and healthy."
"You don't get enough protein."
"You don't eat enough."
"It's a waste not to eat good food."
"How will you ever learn to like things if you don't try them?"
"You'll grow up big and strong if you eat those beans."
"You won't get dessert if you don't eat that liver."

"Think of all the hungry children in the poor countries."
"That food will give you lots of energy."
"Finish your dinner or I'll send you to bed."
"You liked it the last time we had it."
"One taste, just for me."
"I made it just for you."
"You're old enough to expand your tastes a little bit."
"Eat it because I love you."

We know that some of these lines are guilt trips that our parents use because they feel desperate and really think that if we don't eat those turnips (or eggs or broccoli or eggplant) we won't grow strong and healthy. We wish parents wouldn't use these lines and would just let us eat the way we want to eat. We also wish they'd come up with some more creative lines.

Sugar tends to be a big area of concern for parents and we can understand this concern. We don't think sugar is the best thing for anyone — including kids — to eat a lot of, but we like it anyway. Nate said, "I think a kid's intake of sugar should be limited so that the kid will not get fat or get a lot of cavities. The best way to help a kid not to eat so much sugar is to limit the amount that is kept around the house."

Joachim agrees and also thinks "sugar hypes kids up and then makes them tired. Parents should only have sweet things around for kids after dinner." Families should have rules about sugar and candy and they should be followed by the kids and the parents. As Jasanne said, "A child's attitude should be against junk food. Although it tastes great, you really should look at the facts."

Snacking in between meals is also an issue for kids and parents. In general, we think kids should set their own policies about snacking, as long as they are not refusing to eat their meals because of overeating on snacks. Nathan told us about his family's snack policy: "I think the best policy for snacking in between meals is to have one snack about two hours before dinner and that is all. This is my family's policy and I think it's the best."

Mindy thinks that one snack after school and one snack right before bed is a reasonable policy. She said, "My family's policy is one snack after school. I don't want a snack right before bed so I like my family's policy."

Sometimes families can solve dietary issues together. Kris told us about how her family dealt with drinking too much soda: "In my house we always used to have a big bottle of Coke in the refrigerator. One day, my father said we weren't allowed to have Coke in the house anymore because we were drinking at least two or three glasses of Coke a day — each of us. That's a lot of caffeine! We haven't had a Coke for about one week now and we all realize what a bunch of Coke-a-holics we are!"

Parents sometimes go on fad diets or all of a sudden want to bring a special kind of food into the house. Some parents go on health food kicks and try to force us to eat all this strange kind of food. Kama had this happen with her mother: "I remember, a couple of years ago, my mother used to be a real health nut and we used to have only health food in the house and *no* junk food. I thought it was really gross!"

When a parent or a kid needs to lose weight, it's important for everyone to cooperate and be helpful. This means not eating a lot of sugary foods in front of them or saying things like "Do you want some root beer now?" Some of us have had good experiences dieting with our parents' help. Nathan told us, "Last Christmas, I weighed about a hundred and thirty-nine pounds and my waist was thirty-four inches, so my mom and I decided to put me on a weight-loss program. We made a contract that said what I would eat for a whole week. After a month of this, I had lost twenty pounds!"

There are some foods that both kids and parents seem to think are good for kids to eat and that kids enjoy eating. We made a list of these because, if your parent starts to tell you that you only eat lousy food and you should eat more okra, you can tell them that you like some of these foods:

- apple juice
- baked potatoes
- bread (plain and garlic)
- carrots
- cheeses (certain types)
- chicken
- corn
- fish (some kinds)
- grape juice
- hamburger
- hot dogs
- lamb chops
- lobster
- milk
- orange juice
- pies
- rice
- salad
- soups (some kinds)
- spaghetti
- steak
- turkey
- veal

Dinnertime

Dinnertime is often a good time for families to get together and talk about what everyone has been doing all day at school or at work. Sometimes problems come up around dinnertime — fights over manners, kinds of foods, watching television. Parents might be in a lousy mood at dinner because they have had a rough day; kids should keep this in mind and try to behave.

All of us feel that families should get together for dinner regularly. Josh said, "If families never have dinner together, they tend not to talk enough. Dinner is often considered a good time for families to talk about problems, too. For example, a common answer to big questions, such as 'Can I get a dog?' or 'Can I have a bigger allowance?' is often 'Let's discuss it over dinner.' If there isn't a dinner to discuss it over, then these issues can turn into fights later on." Because dinnertime is often the only time for families to all be together, we think that kids should co-operate and make sure this is a good time for everyone.

The time set for dinner can vary greatly from household to household. In our class, it varies from 5:00 to 9:00. We think that dinner should take place when everyone is home and hungry. Of course, whoever is preparing the meal should have the major say in when it has to be ready. Some of us think it's a good idea for a family to set the same time for dinner every night, because then it's easy for the kids to know when to come home. Others of us feel okay about flexible dinner hours.

It's important for people to talk at the dinner table and we generally think it's not a good idea to watch television during dinner (except on special occasions) or read newspapers. We feel that the dinner conversation should be appropriate for mealtimes. David suggests, "People shouldn't talk about slugs or things like that." Josh says, "Talking about gross things over food is offensive — especially dissection of frogs, insects, or worms, or incidents of massive bloodshed."

Josh also thinks that " 'What happened in school today?' would be an okay topic, although very unoriginal and, day after day, would get monotonous. If kids feel comfortable talking personally to parents, your social life could be an interesting topic." Gillian thinks that just everyone talking about what happened during the day is a good idea.

The mealtime chores should be shared between members of the family. For example, the kids could set and clear the table and the parents could make the food. Some

Be patient with little brothers and sisters at the dinner table.

of us like it that our families rotate the jobs, so no one gets really bored with what they have to do each night.

Manners can be a big issue between parents and kids. We talked about what manners we thought were fair for parents to expect kids to follow and what manners we thought were not fair. Mike felt that the following rules should be followed by kids:

no burping at the table
eat with a fork, not with fingers
no disgusting noises or gestures
no throwing food

He also said, "Other, less important manners, such as 'no elbows on the table' should be learned for use at fancy dinners and things like that, but they are sort of dumb to be used at every meal."

Gillian thinks the following are bad habits for kids (or parents) to use at the dinner table:

burping
eating with mouth open
talking with mouth full
playing with food
eating with hands
brushing hair
gobbling food
feeding pets
throwing food

It's also a good idea to use a napkin and try to keep most of your food on your plate or in your mouth.

It's important for older brothers and sisters to be patient with little kids at the table. David told us, "When I eat dinner with my family, my brother always throws his food and gets in trouble. I don't like this, because it puts my parents in a bad mood." We think that both parents and older siblings need to be patient with the younger kids and help them behave.

Sometimes parents like to have fancy meals and kids don't like that. We suggest that you discuss the matter and reach some kind of compromise. Mike told us, "My mom and I are always getting into fights about dinnertime. She wants to have sit-down meals with candlelight and all that stuff. It drives me crazy!"

It's important for both kids and parents to work to make dinner a good time to be together.

Fads

Parents don't seem to mind most fads, because they know that they're not very important, and that, sometimes in just a few weeks, we will not be interested in the fads anymore. The kinds of fads that are generally not liked by our parents are the kinds that can be harmful to children.

Some of the fads we've enjoyed are video games, skateboarding, BMX bikes, Walkman radios, roller skates, certain hairstyles (including Mohawks), Ocean Pacific clothing, leather bands and studs, Dungeons and Dragons, Preppies, Valley Girls, designer jeans, and certain musical trends.

One of the reasons kids get into fads is that older role models often give us the idea that the fads are cool. Kids sometimes enjoy them, also, because lots of fads *are* fun, like BMX bicycles or skateboarding.

Kids enjoy fads like BMX bikes and skateboards.

Kids need to be reasonable about fads — especially when money is involved. Janet, a girl we know, followed the Valley Girl fad. She did the whole bit — the clothes, the voice, everything. The voice was all right with her mother, but the money she spent on clothing made her mother very angry. They talked about it, agreed on setting a limit on the clothing, and then everything was fine.

Andre was into roller-skating. He enjoyed it so much that he would even roller-skate up and down the hall at home. His mom got so mad that she told him never to do it again or she'd take the skates away. He still takes the skates everywhere he goes, but he stopped riding in the halls.

We don't think anyone should make a big deal about fads, since they tend to be harmless and a lot of fun for kids, even if the parents and the other adults think they're kind of strange. If you have problems with parents because of a fad, explain why you enjoy it and remind your parents that it probably won't last very long. That should make them feel better about it.

Friends

It makes life a lot easier if your parents like your friends, especially when it comes to having friends over to play or having sleepovers and other parties. It is a difficult situation if your parent doesn't approve of the friendship. All of us like our parents to get to know our friends in a casual, relaxed sort of way and feel comfortable with them.

When we have friends over to play, we prefer that our parents act normal and generally leave us on our own. As David put it, "When I have a friend come over, I prefer my dad or mom to just act normal, say hi, and let us do what we want to do. I wouldn't like it if my mother or father kept asking the kid questions and embarrassing either the kid or me." One of the bad things for a parent to do when a friend is over is to talk about the guest's private life based on what their child has told them. This could make it look like their child is telling the friend's secrets to the parent.

One boy in our class said, "I would like my parents to be more flexible than usual, so that if one of my friends does something stupid, my parents wouldn't explode on the spot. Some of my friends get scared to be anywhere near my dad because he yells so much." We think that this is a situation that definitely needs some improvement and the father needs to find a way to control his temper, especially in front of friends. When your friends are afraid of your parent, they might avoid coming over to play or they might give you a lot of pity, which you don't want.

What should parents do if they don't approve of your friends? They should sit down and talk about it. In most cases that we've seen, the friend isn't as bad as the parent thinks. If the friend actually *is* that bad, usually the kid won't be friends with him or her for that long. If the child still wants to stay friends with the other child, they should be allowed to, although they should take into account their parent's feelings.

When parents meet your friends for the first time and don't like them from the start, they shouldn't act any differently than if they liked them. Afterward, they should sit down and tell you. We really don't like it when parents are mean to a friend of ours, but we think it's fine for parents to limit the kinds of things you can do with that friend that involves a parent. For example, they might ask you not to take them on family outings or not have them sleep over so much, but they should only do this when they *really* don't like a friend. Sometimes, if you talk about it, you and your parents can work something out, and they might begin to understand why you like this person.

When a friend is over, it's sometimes fun for a parent to join you for certain kinds of activities. We usually prefer for the parent to leave us alone while we're playing games, but it would be fine, once in a while, for a parent to play ball with us. Elizabeth likes it when her aunt helps make a pizza. She doesn't like it when her aunt drops in every five minutes, just to check up on things.

Kris said, "Some good things to do with a parent and your friend would be to go to a movie or some kind of festival, or maybe a museum. It would be bad to go to a place that the kids don't enjoy at all, just because the parent says that it would be very interesting and 'educational.' "

When a friend is over for a meal, you might feel a little awkward and wonder whether you should talk with your friend, talk with your parents, or try to talk with everyone. Parents usually try to help out by leading the conversation, and this is fine, as long as they don't get embarrassing or too personal. Macy likes it when parents "ask about school, family, hobbies, and friends. Although these are rather boring subjects, I think they are the most popular among adults." Elizabeth agrees with Macy.

David told us a story about when a friend of his came over for dinner: "My friend didn't like what we were eating, so he wasn't eating. My mother asked him why he wasn't hungry and he said he didn't eat anything without salt. We got him salt and he finally ate the food. I was very embarrassed. Later, he told me he didn't like steak." It's hard to say something like this at the dinner table, because you don't want your friend's parents to make a big fuss and make some other food, or feel insulted, but you don't want to eat the food either.

Mike told us this story: "This summer, when my mother and I were staying in London, a friend came to visit and we went out for dinner. We walked around looking for a restaurant and finally found a pub. I rejected it, saying I didn't want pub food. We walked around a while and found a French restaurant. Grudgingly, I went inside. What I really wanted was Chicken McNuggets, not steak tartare. Anyway, we went inside and got the menu. I looked over the selection and said that I would eat later, when we got home.

" 'Why?' my mother demanded.

" 'I don't like French food!' I told her and I didn't.

" 'Look at Natey. He's not grumbling. Why can't you act like that?!' she replied.

" 'If you like the way he eats so much, why don't you adopt him!' That line reminded me of times other people's parents had done this to them, with me as the 'perfect' friend.

" 'Mom, why are all you parents so nearsighted? When a kid is around a friend's family, they act polite. When a kid is around their own parents, they act normal. That's why it seems like all my friends are more polite!'

"After a long talk, we ate dinner, which, by the way, I enjoyed."

Parents should be very careful about comparing us to our friends, both because they don't really get to see the friends at their normal behavior and because this kind of comparison is not fair and is harmful to kids.

It's nice when your friends like your parents. Macy said, "Once, I had a friend over who had divorced parents and was pretty upset about it, although she didn't show it. My mother talked to her and made her feel much better. Later she told me that she wished that my mother was hers. That made me feel proud, but sorry for the girl."

Joachim told us this story about his father and some of the kids he hangs out with: "Whenever my father picks me up at the YMCA, I'm usually playing video games with some kids watching me. Once someone said something extremely racist, so my father talked to the kid about it. After that, the kid and his friends would stare at me a lot. But it didn't bother me because they were all racist pigs."

If you are staying at a friend's house, we recommend that you try to behave and not complain about everything that happens. Sometimes problems and embarrassing situations come up, but you should pretend it's not a big deal and you shouldn't tell anyone else about it. If you don't behave or if you act like a grump, it can be rough on your friend. Macy told us another story: "I remember one disastrous weekend when I invited a really obnoxious friend over — though at the time I didn't know she was obnoxious. The kid complained about everything from the pizza we ate to the sleeping bag. She got on my mother's nerves, so there was a real shaky relationship between them." When this happens, you can't wait till the visit is over and your friend is gone.

Sometimes parents are in a bad mood when a friend is visiting, yet they're able to handle it well. Elizabeth had a friend over one afternoon and they were talking in her room. She told us, "My aunt came home and she was in a really bad mood and didn't even say hello. I went into her room to ask her what was wrong. All she said was that if I wanted my friend to spend the night, I would have to cook dinner, wash dishes, and clean the den. I went into the other room and started cleaning, and she came out and said that she was sorry and I didn't have to clean."

Some kids we know have a different problem. Their

problem is that their parents never get to meet their friends or that they don't feel they have good enough friends to bring home. Some kids don't bring friends home because they are embarrassed about their home or their neighborhood. Bringing friends home is a good way to make them feel closer to you and, if you're afraid to bring them home because you don't think your parents will welcome them, let your parents know. They'll probably feel bad about that and go out of their way to let you know that your friends are welcome.

Homework

We like it when our parents are concerned about our education and take an active role in making sure that our homework and schoolwork are going well. We like them to show that they care about us and that if we get into trouble they will help us out. Although it is good to have parents who are interested in what you are doing in school, it is not good when parents become overly involved or nag you about it.

We've thought about how parents can help out with homework. First of all, it is helpful if parents show that they care about whether or not we do our homework. Some parents don't seem to care at all or are too busy with their lives to stay on top of this situation. This is not good, especially for a young child (say in second or third grade), and it encourages the kid not to care about homework. Parents can also help with specific homework that you might have. They could help with math if they are able to understand the problem themselves. They could also help proofread written work, and correct the spelling and grammar errors. It's also helpful if parents take you to libraries and other places when you have to do research work, since it's sometimes hard to find a way to get there yourself.

Parents are usually interested in tests. They like it when kids do well on tests. It helps for parents to care about the test *before* it is taken. For example, parents could help us study for a test by asking us questions about the information that might be on the test. Then if the kid does poorly on the test, the parent might understand why — for example, if you studied the wrong thing or if the test was just very difficult.

When parents are helping with our homework, we don't necessarily want them to do it all themselves. Some parents try to help you and then they just do the work themselves and don't teach you how to do it. It's more helpful if a parent gives you clues and hints rather than tells you the answer. It's also helpful if they are very, very patient and explain things in simple terms. Some parents we know get easily frustrated and lose their tempers and start yelling when we don't understand. This makes us feel dumb and embarrassed and it defeats the whole purpose of getting help. We understand that it's sometimes hard for parents to control their tempers, but we really think it's important.

Parents can also help by making sure that kids have a good place to work on their homework and the necessary equipment. It would also be nice if a parent would encourage us not to do the homework while we were watching TV, but they shouldn't make a big deal about it, or about the radio being on. The best a parent can do is to monitor kids lightly when homework is being done and to be available for help as needed. The parent should not be constantly nagging or looking over the child's shoulder.

Homework should not become a large household issue.

If a student is doing badly in school, or not getting homework finished, the parent should do something about it. Unfortunately, many parents' first reaction is to yell and scream and punish the child. Some of them feel that it's a reflection on them if the child does poorly — as if the parent is being judged on the child's schoolwork. If a child has problems, Caleb thinks the parent should "talk it over with the child and find out what's really going on. Then make appointments and talk to the child's teacher — if it is something serious that needs to be discussed. Parents should not over-react or stomp around about it or make the child feel badly without real reason."

If it comes to punishments because the child is being lazy, Kris thinks that "they should have phone calls cut down, limit the number of friends coming over, and tell them to come straight home from school and do schoolwork." In general, however, talking about it and trying to solve the problem is better than punishing for most kids.

If we are doing well in school, parents should make sure we know it, and they should tell us they are happy about it and say things like "Keep it up!" They should be careful about how much praise they give. If your parent is too flattering, you could get an inflated ego. We don't think that parents should shower kids with gifts or toys or spend a lot of money on us because we do well in school. If parents are unreasonable and begin to compare their child to other children and say things like "You're smarter than Carmen and Lily," then the child may start to feel superior to other kids and get a little conceited. Watch out for this.

When it's time to get a report card, parents should read it carefully and discuss it with the child. They should give their honest reactions but not get angry or over-react.

They should tell how they feel about it, what they expected of the child, what they disagree with, and how to solve any problems. Parents should work with the child to find solutions to problems. And parents should never compare one child's report card with another child's — especially a brother or sister. Kris's parents read her report card and she told us, "They just act calm and cool. Then they talk to me about how they feel about my schoolwork."

It sometimes feels funny to us when our parents are having a conference with our teacher. It's strange to know that some people are talking about you with you not there. After the conference, kids should ask their parents what was said and make sure that anything bad is explained. From what we can tell, most conferences seem pretty boring to us and we're glad that we're not there.

We also like it when parents are involved in school activities when they are expected to be — coming to school events, watching us when we're in plays or doing some special activities, and showing that they are involved in our schooling. This can get out of hand, too, but we like parents to be there when there are parent/child events. It's especially nice that some fathers are involved in these, although mothers tend to get more involved than fathers.

Movies

Movie-going can become a big part of your life, especially as you get to be a teenager. Before this time, most of the movies you see will be with your family or with your friends' families, but once you are about twelve or thirteen, you'll start going to movies with your friends. This can be fun, but some parents disagree with you about which movies you can see with your friends. It's a lot easier for them to have control over the movies you watch when you go with them.

When we go to the movies with our parents, we sometimes have a hard time deciding which movies we should see. This should be decided by talking about it and compromising. Often there will be at least one movie that everyone wants to see. Sometimes the kids should go to a movie that the parent wants to see and other times the parent should go along with the kid.

Most of us enjoy going to the movies with our parents and the rest of the family. Ana said, "I like going to the movies with my family because it makes me feel closer to them." Kate said, "Sometimes I like to go with my whole family, but usually our family doesn't all go to the movies together for four main reasons: my little brother, we all have different movie tastes, my mother hates going to movies, and it's too expensive for four people to all go at the same time." We think that it might be a good idea for there to be family or group rates at movies, so that it isn't so expensive to take the whole group.

Sometimes parents won't take you to a movie you want to see — because they don't like the movie or because of the movie rating or because of their schedule. Jonathan told us, "I wanted to see *The Wall* but my mom wouldn't let me. We talked it over and finally she let me see it." Talking can sometimes change a parent's mind about a movie.

Joachim has difficulty going to R-rated movies. He said, "Whenever I want to go to a movie that is rated R, my stepmother won't take me because she feels it will affect my growing up. It's a bummer because I don't get to go to a lot of movies I want to see."

Josh also has trouble with the movie rating system. He told us, "Unless you are religious (very, very religious), and can't stand to hear swears being said or see sex in the movies, I think the ratings system is on the brink of uselessness. I wish it weren't there, because it stops me from being able to go to the movies with my friends. Since all the good movies are rated R, we have to search around for a decent PG movie, which is a pain. What do they think is going to happen if we hear a few beeps or bleeps in the movies? Do they think they'll corrupt us? We use them enough anyway!"

Kate has some problems with the ratings system. She said, "I think a lot of time that the system is a little out of whack. For instance, when they rate a movie PG because there is one swear in it, or when they rate a movie R because of so-called nudity. I also think that X-rated movies are gross and I will never see one again (we saw one on cable TV at my party one year). They are disgusting, pornographic movies that portray a perverted view of sex and people. I can see no reason why people get pleasure out of them."

Joachim thinks the rating system is pretty good and most of us feel the same way.

Going to the movies with your parents can cause some problems. Some of them are relatively easy to deal with. Elizabeth told us, "One problem I face every time I go to the movies is where to sit. I like to sit up close, but my aunt prefers to sit farther back. We like to sit together, but I always end up sitting way in the back." Other problems involve how much candy to get, whether to sit with your friends or your parents or both, and disagreeing about whether you liked the movie or not.

Sometimes you can get embarrassed going to the movies with a parent. Jesse told us, "One time, I went to a movie with my mom, and we were watching a preview for *The Shining*, and the preview was of a mildly scary part of the movie. My mom started screaming — *frantically*. I don't like going to scary movies with my family."

Most of us select movies based on a combination of factors. We read the reviews in the newspapers, and we ask our friends who have seen the movies. Sometimes we go to see a movie anyway, even though our friends and our parents tell us it's not a good movie. In general, we think that seeing a movie with a parent is a good experience and can give you some things to talk about that keep your mind off the problems or disputes you might have.

Parents Staying Out Late

Children of different ages will react differently to parents staying out late. Little kids, even with baby-sitters, might be scared if their parents stay out late and they might worry that something happened to them. Older kids might enjoy the time in the house alone. As Macy put it, "I think kids my age would love it when their parents stay out late, because they can talk on the phone all night and blast the stereo."

In general, regardless of the age of the children, we think it's important for parents to tell them when they expect to be home and then try to get home close to that time. Some parents stay out late to go to a lecture or to see a movie. Others are on dates or going to a party or working late or on a business trip. Some parents are out later than expected because they are having a good time and they forget about the time. We know some parents who try to pack too many activities into one night and always come home too late.

It's scary to be home alone and hear spooky sounds.

Some kids feel neglected when their parents stay out too late all the time. Other kids react differently. Matt said, "When I was younger, I used to be proud to be able to stay home without my parents there. Now I usually don't care."

If you are an older child who doesn't need a baby-sitter anymore, you might find that you still get scared sometimes when your parents are out late. There might be noises in your building, or a phony phone call might be made. You might see a scary television show and get spooked. Here is a list of some of the things we do, when our parents are not home and we get scared:

phone a close friend or neighbor
whistle
turn on the radio or TV very loudly
call up your parents (if you know where they are)
do a lot of homework
pretend that the parent is in the other room and try to go to sleep
count sheep
play a fun game that takes concentration
use some loud kitchen appliances (if you're allowed to)

If your parents are frequently out late, or come home later than they tell you, you might want to sit down and talk with them about it. Let them know how it makes you feel. It might help to think of a way that will help them get home on time, like buying them a watch on their birthday.

Parents are not the only ones who sometimes stay out late. Sometimes kids are expected to be home at a certain time and they are late. This gets parents worried and upset and sometimes they are also very angry and punish us. Parents should be very clear about what time a child's curfew is and then, if the child is late just once, remind him or her. If the child is late a lot, the parent should probably take some action. A good punishment should be set, but not a severe one. If the child is just a couple of minutes late, the parent might talk to the child, without making a big deal about it.

Pets

Before a family decides to get a pet, they should carefully consider all the issues about having a pet: who will feed it, walk it (if necessary), clean the cage, and so on. They should make sure they really want a pet and that it will be okay to have this pet along with any other animals they already have at home. It's important for kids and parents to think very carefully about whether they are enthusiastic enough to take good care of a pet, because if they're not, they probably won't take good care of it and it will die or be mistreated. This is a bad thing to have to live with on your conscience.

Responsibilities for the pet should be discussed and agreed upon by the whole family. If it is the child's pet, then the child is the primary person responsible for its care. If it is a cat or dog, the child should make sure it can go outside each day and should clean the litter box, and pet it or pay attention to it a little bit. The adult in the family should be willing to make sure the child does all of the work involved with the pet and sometimes offer to help out. They should also be willing to be responsible for the pet if the child is sick or away from home.

We thought about what kinds of pets parents like to have and what kinds of pets kids like to have. Kate thinks that "most parents seem to prefer small, clean, easy-to-take-care-of pets, such as hamsters, gerbils, fish, guinea pigs, birds, and occasionally, cats and dogs."

Mike told us, "The type of pet a child likes depends on the personality of the child — some like Saint Bernards and some like canaries." He agrees that most parents seem to like small, quiet pets like gerbils and hamsters.

Tanya thinks this preference depends on the parents and kids involved. She said, "Generally, I have noticed that parents don't like small little rodents and prefer to have a dog to a rodent. Their favorite pets are easy-to-take-care-of ones that don't make too much noise — particularly fish. Kids generally like rodents and dogs."

We've also noticed that parents and kids sometimes disagree about what to name a pet. Some parents don't realize what a big issue this is for kids and insist on naming the pet themselves without any input or suggestions from the children. We don't think this is a good idea, mainly because pets are very important to kids and we think the name matters a lot. If one member of the family "owns" the pet, then that person should decide on the name. If it is a family pet, everyone should sit down and talk about it.

John came up with a couple of suggestions for naming pets as a family. He said, "You could brainstorm a whole

Kids like cuddly pets.

bunch of names and then take a vote. For small pets (rats, hamsters, etc.), you can put all the names you have in a circle and put the pet in the center and see which one the pet picks."

We've all had problems come up about pets. Jonathan told us about a rabbit his sister had: "My sister once had a rabbit that lived in the whole upstairs. This was great having it there all the time, but after a while we noticed that she was eating our clothes and chewing the wires. My mother said that we'd have to get rid of her. My sister disagreed. She said, 'It's not so hard — just get new clothes.' My mom didn't think this was the best answer so we got rid of her (the bunny, not my sister)."

Kris was able to get a puppy, even though her brothers didn't like the idea. She said, "When I went to camp, there was a really cute little dog there that I liked so much, I wanted to have it — or at least a dog like it. When my mom saw it, she liked it too. We told my dad and my brothers about it and they all said 'No!' Finally, my mom talked my dad into getting a dog, although my brothers were still saying 'No!' One afternoon I came home with a little Shih Tzu. My mom and I thought she was cute, my brothers thought she was ugly, and my dad didn't say anything. Now everyone in our family thinks she's cute and we all love her a lot."

Kate had a similar situation in her family. "When my horse (who is now only half mine) was living with us, I wanted a guinea pig, also," Kate said. "My parents said no, a horse was enough to take care of. For a while I stopped asking, but then I started pestering for a guinea pig again. This time they said that, if I could show them that I could take perfect care of the horse and still have some time left over to take care of a guinea pig, I could have one. So, for three weeks, I took perfect care of the horse and still had time left over. I got the guinea pig and still kept and loved my horse."

Not all situations turn out with parents and kids feeling good about the pet. Last year, Jake's grandpa came for a visit from New York and took Jake to a pet store. Jake told us, "He bought me two lizards. My mom was not thrilled with this, so we made a deal. If either of the lizards ever escaped, my mom would check into an expensive hotel at my grandpa's expense."

When a pet dies, it's important for the parent to be honest and open with the child and explain things and not try to hide it. Kids will have different reactions to a pet dying, but parents can help the most if they listen to the child and don't tell them there's anything wrong with their feelings. Josh told us about his family's pet's death: "Recently, we found out that the cat we had had for five years had a tumor and had to be 'put to sleep.' My mom took it to the vet's and she and my brother kept the cat company while it was killed. They left after it was all over, leaving the cat there. That night, my brother got upset and wanted to bury the cat. My mom called up the vet and we buried it the next day."

Losing a pet or having it run away can also be difficult. Jesse thinks that if a pet gets lost, the family should look for it, ask neighbors if they've seen it, or even put out a reward for the pet's return. Stephen told us about losing one of his pets: "I had a hamster named Teddy who escaped from his cage one day. I looked all over the place for him, but I still couldn't find Teddy. I called my mother downstairs and we both began to look and we still couldn't find him. I hope he got outside and led a strong and healthy life because I never found Teddy."

One of the things that might help our parents understand some of the problems that come up with pets and why we are often so concerned about them is if we could make them see what kids like about pets. Jesse thinks that many kids have pets that are very special to them and "are actually good friends with them." Mike told us that "pets will always listen to you, even when you've had a fight with one of your parents or friends."

Jake told us, "I would just love to get a frog, but I think parents just don't understand the pleasure of seeing your frog hop around." Other things kids get from pets are love, understanding, and comfort.

Mindy thinks, "Children like to have someone to share griefs with. They like to have a friend who almost never gets mad at them. This can be a pet."

We think Kate sums up the appeal pets have for many kids and may point out why kids relate to pets differently than parents do: "Having a thing that's alive to care for and be responsible for is like what a parent is to a child. It's kind of like being a parent for a kid to have a pet, and much more satisfying than playing parent to a doll."

The whole family should agree about taking care of pets.

Religion and Politics

Religion and politics can become an issue between a parent and a child for a few reasons. If the parent, for example, has strong religious beliefs that the child doesn't agree with, they might argue about whether the child has to go to church or synagogue with the rest of the family. If the parent is very active politically, the child might feel that the parent cares more about the president than about the child. There can be a lot of fights around the dinner table between the parent and the child about politics and religion — including such questions as "Is there a God?" or "Who should I vote for?"

We've experienced some of these problems ourselves. Mike's mom tries desperately to get him to go to Quaker meeting but he always refuses to go. Elizabeth's father is Episcopalian and her stepmother is Presbyterian and when they married they couldn't decide which religion to stay with so there were arguments in the family about it. One child in our class gets into a lot of political arguments with his father and sometimes his father argues with the child's friends as well.

In general, we don't care whether our parents are very religious or very political. We feel that this is a personal decision they can make. We sometimes see some good things in this. Jonathan told us, "My father is a heavy socialist activist and, sometimes, I find it hard to believe in the same things he does. I try to see things his way and that helps a little." One benefit of having a political or a religious parent is that you can become very well educated on a particular subject. This could help you later in life.

Josh told us this story: "Once I had a friend over who is more political than most of my other friends. He wanted to light a single candle in the window in support of Solidarity. My parents were not opposed to this, but my father somehow included other politics into it. My friend then said that this (meaning Solidarity) was Reagan's and the Pope's politics — he is more conservative than I am, and much more conservative than my parents. My father exploded at that point since he can't stand both Reagan and the Pope. (I can't stand them either, but I controlled myself.) My father yelled at my friend. I thought that this was obnoxious so I yelled at him and went upstairs with my friend."

We think it's fine for parents to have strong views, but they need to make sure that they don't shove their views down their child's throat. It is one thing to be politically involved and it's another thing to force a child to have the same point of view. We think it is okay to expose children to politics or religion but they have to be allowed to make their own decisions about these things.

Sleepovers

Having a friend sleep over at your house or sleeping over at a friend's house are important to kids. All of us agree that sleepovers are usually fun for kids, but we had different ideas about why we like them so much. Joachim thinks that "for some children, it is an important chance to get to know their friend outside of school." David said that one of the fun parts of a sleepover is "you get away from your parents for a night," and Jonathan thinks that it's good to see a friend at your home or his home because "it's a much more personal atmosphere than being at school or at other popular hangouts."

Unfortunately, many parents think that their child's friend sleeping over will be a lot of bother for them. Most of us can't see how it can create a lot of work for the parents. Also, some parents are reluctant to allow their child to spend the night at a friend's house if they don't know or don't approve of the family of the other child. Most parents don't like sleepovers on school nights and we can see their point. It's hard to go to bed on time when a friend is over, and at least on weekends you have the chance to sleep late.

Kids and parents should talk about sleepovers in advance and establish any rules and set the bedtime hour. Parents should be flexible and know that kids really enjoy having a friend sleep over. It's okay for parents to make rules such as no overly loud music, no making a total mess of the house, and no screaming. Some rules that we think are not suitable for sleepovers are that you can only play quiet games, that you can't talk after lights out, and that you can't have snacks. Kids need to be cooperative with their parents when a friend sleeps over, and when more than one friend sleeps over, the child should make sure everything is cleaned up in the morning.

One of the best parts about having a friend sleep over is that it's one of the few times you get to spend in your house with someone who is around your same age. There are lots of things that are fun to do with friends that you don't necessarily like to do with brothers and sisters. David said that, during sleepovers, "I like to have pillow fights and also call up people on the telephone. Watching TV is also fun." Kate likes "going to the movies or out to dinner, or doing things that you normally don't do because there is no one your age to do them with." Jesse said, "Some fun things to do are listen to music, talk on the phone, watch TV, play games, and stay up late."

One thing we don't recommend is for parents to call up the place where you're sleeping over and make sure you've done things like brush your teeth and wash your face. This can be embarrassing. If parents want to call up the house ahead of time, just to make sure that some adult is going to be home to supervise things, that's fine. But we don't recommend other calls, except maybe to find out if you need a ride home the next morning.

When a friend sleeps over, sometimes problems will come up and it's important that both the child and the parent handle the problem properly. Jesse told us this story: "One time a friend slept over and we were drinking Coke and I dropped my glass and broke it, so my mom got really mad and accused us of fooling around too much. She made us stay in my room the rest of the night. I feel that my mom didn't have to go out of her way to get so mad at me just for breaking a glass."

Joachim had a problem with bedtimes when his friend slept over: "About two years ago I had a friend over for the night and my mom made us go to bed early. Since he was a couple of years older than me, it was quite embarrassing. My feeling is that, if my mom made us go to bed, she could have let us at least talk for a while." We feel that parents and kids should plan bedtimes for sleepovers even before a friend is invited over.

Tanya told us, "Once when I had a friend sleep over, we got into a fight. It wasn't anything that we couldn't handle ourselves, but my parents butted in and, without listening to our stories, they took my friend's side. I think that they should have stayed out of it and minded their own business and only entered the situation if we couldn't handle it ourselves."

It's important to make sure your parent doesn't overreact to problems when a friend is over and that difficult

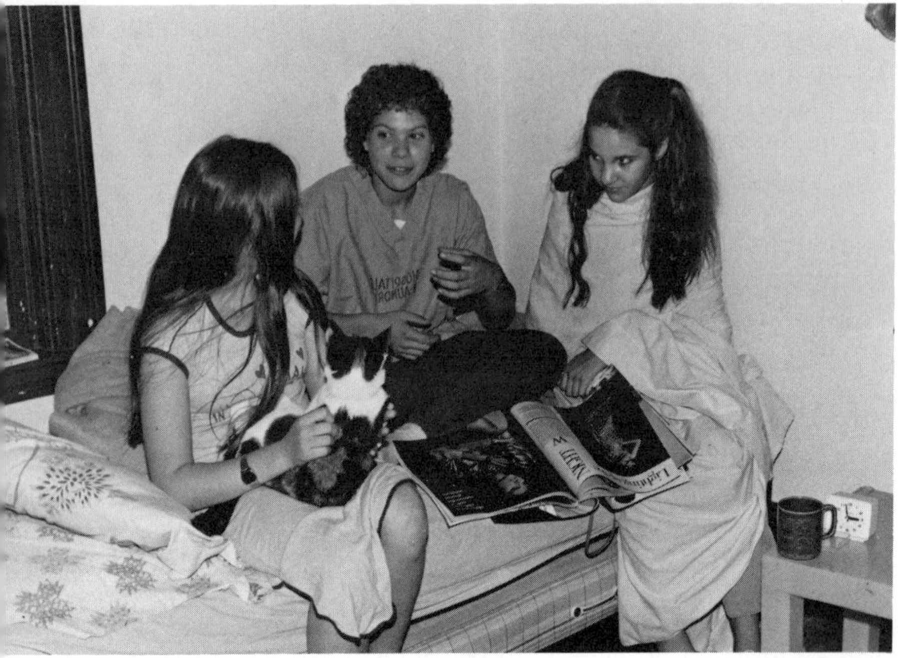

Sleepovers can be a lot of fun.

situations are handled properly. Jesse told us, "One time I slept over a friend's house. We played for a while and then, all of a sudden, his dad came in and said, 'Because you didn't do your chores, Jesse is going to have to go home now.' My mom had to come and pick me up. I don't think that he should have done this, just because my friend didn't do his chores."

One of the nice things about sleeping over at a friend's house is you get to know their parents and brothers and sisters a little bit. It's also kind of nice for your parents to get to meet your friends when you have them over. It makes them feel like you have chosen good people to spend your time with and they might worry about you a little bit less.

Television

Many kids and parents have disagreements about television: which shows to watch, how much time kids can watch television, whether or not some things are bad for kids to see. In talking about problems that come up with our parents regarding television, we realized that all kids don't like the same shows on television and that some kids don't really like watching TV very much. Most of us, however, tend to watch a lot of television and really enjoy it.

Nathan watches a lot of sports and movies on television, although his mom wants him to watch educational shows like *Nova*. Gillian likes watching comedies and mysteries and her favorite television show is *M*A*S*H*. Mike likes to watch science shows and usually his parents don't care what he watches. Sometimes, if there is a show on TV that they think he should see, they ask him to watch it and he usually does. Kate rarely watches television and told us, "I only watch TV when I have nothing else to do or if there's a movie on that I want to watch."

We talked about how much time is appropriate for kids to watch television and what shows are good for kids to see. We think that this is something that should be discussed within the family. Caleb said, "Both parents and children should be involved in the decision, and it should involve what the child wants to watch but also what the adult feels is a reasonable amount of time for the child to watch. It shouldn't be an outrageous amount of time and the TV shouldn't be on just to be on."

Kate thinks that there should be no need for parents to set a limit on the amount of TV that a kid watches. She told us, "Children should not have so much free time that they spend three or four hours a day in front of the TV. If they do, parents and children should look into after-school activities for the kids."

Josh thinks that, if the children are responsible, they should be allowed to watch without rules. If the kids watch television so long that they hardly do anything else, he thinks the parents should make some rules — maybe limiting it to two or three hours a day.

Stephen feels kids and parents should decide together on the right amount of time for watching TV. He said, "All the child's homework should be done and all the child's chores for the day should be finished before TV is watched."

Often families get into conflicts because there is only one television set and several people want to watch different shows. In some families, it's the kid who loses out and the parents are the ones who get to watch their show. They tell you this is because they bought the TV set, or because they've had a hard day at work, or that it's just because they're the parents and they're in charge. We think that other methods should be used to determine what shows are watched. Caleb thinks that, in this situation, "obviously someone is going to have to compromise. Although it is important to decide this in the right way, television decisions shouldn't become a big deal. Everyone should decide together and factors such as whether one of the programs will be repeated should be considered. A switching-compromise system might be worked out where one member would compromise and then the other would compromise the next time. Any way it is decided is fine, but if there are always big disagreements, then it might be better not to watch TV at all."

Heather thinks, "If there's a once-in-a-lifetime movie on, and there's a stupid sitcom at the same time, the person who wants to see the movie should get to see it."

Mike and his mother once got into a fight about what TV show they were going to watch. He told us, "The fight ended with me storming out of the room, and since the TV was in the room my mom was in, she got to watch the show she wanted to watch."

A girl we know and her sister found another way to help prevent fights over television shows. "We finally got so tired of arguing that we decided to sit down and make a schedule," she told us. "My sister would watch one show, then I would watch a show of my choice. This worked out well, because we allowed each other to make exceptions and we alternated days."

Compromising seems to be the key to solving these problems. Nate explained, "My mom wanted to watch a show on Channel 2 (public television) and my brother and I wanted to watch a Clint Eastwood movie, so we decided that, if I was able to watch Clint, my mom could watch her show the next time the same kind of problem came up."

Flipping a coin is a solution that Jesse's family has tried. "One time, a few months ago, my sister and I were watching TV," Jesse said. "I wanted to watch *Streets of San Francisco* and she wanted to watch *The Brady Bunch*, so we flipped a coin. She won, so I went biking." If you decide to flip a coin, both people must follow whatever decision comes about and not complain and make a big deal about losing.

Sometimes you can surprise yourself when you end up liking someone else's show that you didn't think you'd enjoy. Gillian said, "I once wanted to watch a show and my parents said I couldn't because they were watching a show. They said I couldn't watch TV unless I watched their show. I watched it and it was pretty good."

Josh thinks it's important to keep in mind that some parents very rarely watch television and some kids watch it all the time. "If the parents want to watch something different from the children's normal television pattern," he said, "the parents should be able to watch. This goes for different members of the family, as well."

Very special television shows should be recognized and respected by the family. Every year when the World Series comes around, Josh's brother wants to watch his normal shows while Josh wants to watch the games. "The situation is always solved, though," Josh said. "My mom gives a lecture to my brother about how the World Series only comes once a year and he can see his programs anytime."

As kids get older — about thirteen or fourteen — their television problems with their parents become less serious, mainly because they are allowed to make their own decisions and their parents don't seem to mind them watching violent shows. Elizabeth also thinks that "the typical teenager probably won't have time to watch TV because of homework and socializing (especially over the telephone)."

Television problems also become less important when kids develop other interests. Kate told us, "A friend of mine used to watch TV a lot. She and her mother always argued about it. Then the girl started taking ballet lessons, which took up a lot of her time, so this solved all their problems. After she became involved in ballet, television did not hold the same appeal for her."

Staying up late to watch TV shows is also a problem for a lot of kids. Parents don't want to extend bedtimes just because we're watching an exciting movie, or a special TV show is about to come on. Caleb told us, "Many times when I would like to watch a TV movie that runs late, my mother and I have 'disagreements' (ahem!) about if I am going to watch till late. Most often I state my arguments and excuses — 'no school tomorrow,' 'I'll go to bed really early tomorrow,' etc. Sometimes I do get to watch, but most of the time, my mother wins and I see part of the movie or none at all. These are resolved more or less like a dictatorship rule. Occasionally, if I'm lucky, I'll get to see the movie (when she feels guilty, maybe), even after I was supposed to be in bed."

We think it's important for parents and kids to find workable ways of resolving their conflicts about television. While all of us would agree that there are good shows and bad shows on television, we have different opinions about which shows fit into each of these categories. We want to find a way to let people watch their shows and, at the same time, not have the television become a major member of the family.

When You Are Unhappy

Kids get into bad moods also — just like parents. Some of the reasons we get into bad moods are: not being able to do something we want to do; having a fight with a parent, sibling, or friend; moving or going to a new school; not doing well on a test; having a pet get sick; being yelled at unfairly. Kids also are unhappy when their parents get divorced or fight a lot, when they have no money, and when they don't feel they have as much status with friends as they would like to have.

Justin told us, "I have been unhappy at times when I am not able to go somewhere that I want to or can't have snacks before dinner. Also, when all my friends are going to the same high school and I have to go to a different one, or when I can't have money for video games, or my baseball team loses, or my friends are mad at me. Sometimes I'm upset when I don't get an assignment in on time, or people are making fun of me (this makes me both mad and unhappy). I also get unhappy and very mad when kids beat me up, or when I forget things on a test that I knew before."

We hope our parents know how to act with us when we are not happy. They should be nice to us, try to understand, and try not to take things out on us. Talking is helpful, but they should not pressure us to talk if we don't want to. Some of us like it a lot when our parents do something to distract us from what's on our mind. It's also nice to do special things like go to a movie or go out to eat. That's a good way to forget your bad mood.

We can think of five things that parents shouldn't do when their kid is unhappy:

1. Don't yell at or be mean to the kid.
2. Don't ignore the situation and pretend you haven't noticed that the child is unhappy, depressed, or angry.
3. Don't make the child feel guilty or wrong for being in a bad mood.
4. Don't tell the kid that he or she shouldn't feel these feelings or is a baby because of them.
5. Don't be excessively cheery, phony, or make too many jokes.

Sometimes kids can take care of themselves when they are not happy. Nate likes to go biking to forget his problems when he is depressed. Mike likes to talk about things when he is sad but also likes to go someplace and get his mind off things after he's talked about it. Jesse told us, "I feel a lot better when my mother feeds me when I'm not happy." He also told us, "When I'm unhappy, I try to get my mind off my troubles by watching cooking shows on TV, like Julia Child's show or *Romagnolis' Kitchen*. This was my friend Nate's idea and it sometimes works." Kama has noticed that some people write down their thoughts or draw pictures when they're not happy.

Sometimes our parents have a hard time understanding

Some kids like to be alone when they are not happy.

how we feel when we're not happy. This varies from child to child. Mike told us, "When I am not happy, I feel like I'm all alone and I depress myself even more by thinking things like 'I'll probably be depressed forever. It's probably just my lot in life.' " Gillian told us that when she is not happy she often feels "very depressed and heavy. I also get a stomachache and my stomach feels very full. I feel like crying very often. And I have a tendency to blame or snap at someone for no reason." When Jamey isn't happy, she told us, "I feel like I'll never be happy or have fun again. I sometimes feel angry at the same time."

It's important for all of us to realize that we sometimes feel unhappy and that it is not the end of the world. It is sometimes difficult to remember this, but it's true. Even when you feel your very worst, you should remember that there will come a time — sometimes in a few minutes and sometimes in a few days — when you will feel happy again. This keeps things in perspective and allows you to stay optimistic.

Our parents have sometimes handled our bad moods well and sometimes not. Macy told us, "One time I got into a rather large and messy argument with a good friend of mine. I was so upset that I was crying, and I went and told my mother. She told me she wasn't going to have any part of it, because I had started it (which was true but at the same time made me feel angry at her and helpless)."

Gillian had a similar situation. "One time, I had just had a fight with a friend. When I got home, my parents noticed I was upset. They sat me down and made me talk about it when I didn't want to. It really made me feel patronized and feel even worse than I did before." Again, we do not recommend forcing children to talk about problems if they don't want to.

Nate's mom once tried to help him feel better and it backfired. He told us, "I was not accepted on the baseball team I wanted to be on and, instead of encouraging me, my mother said, 'You didn't really want to be on the team, did you?' This made me feel horrible."

In some cases, our parents have handled our bad moods very well. Sometimes they've learned what we like them to do and sometimes they are just lucky. Mike told us, "One time, when I thought that I had broken up with my girlfriend, my dad noticed that I was sort of moping around. He asked me what was wrong and we had a long talk about how I felt. Afterward, I felt a lot better."

Joachim's father had a good solution for his depression. Joachim told us, "When I got into a fight with one of my friends and I was depressed, my father took me to a movie and it got my mind off it." Joachim's mom also did a good job of making him feel better in another situation. He told us, "When I went to the doctor's office to get a shot, I was unhappy. So, while the nurse was giving me the shot, my mom was distracting me. That helped a lot."

Parents can help kids deal with very difficult situations that come up. Kate told us about one of these times:

"When I was ten years old and my guinea pig, Ginger, died, my mother was very helpful. First of all, she held me while I cried. Then, about half an hour later, I stopped crying and my sister and I went out to bury Ginger. When we came back in, nobody said anything about Ginger. I was happy about that because I did not really want to talk about it then. Before, when I was crying, my mother explained to me that she probably just got sick and died and that that was common for guinea pigs to do. That night, after dinner, my stepfather, Don, cleaned out the cage and put it in the cellar. I was also happy that I did not have to do that. I stayed downstairs until the cage was put in the cellar, so I never had to see the empty cage and know that Ginger was not there."

Kids need their parents' help when they are not happy and it's important for us to be honest with our parents about what we need. Decide if you want them to hold you or leave you alone, talk to you or avoid the situation. Then let them know how best to deal with you in these moods. This can make the family situation a lot better when bad things are happening.

When Your Parents Are Unhappy

We have noticed that there are many times when our parents are sad, angry, depressed, irritable, disappointed, hostile, or plain "in a bad mood." As we get older, we find better ways of dealing with them when they're in these moods. We think it's important for all kids to learn the signals their parents give off when they're in a bad mood, and to find a way of dealing with the situation that causes a minimum of problems — for the kid and for the parent.

There are many reasons parents may not be happy. Usually, a minor incident can be the cause of these feelings, such as a bad day at work, a fight with a friend or the other parent, forgetting something, or breaking a dish. Other times there are more serious causes, including losing a job, not having enough money, getting kicked out of your apartment, having a relative die, getting a divorce, or having a car accident. Depending on the cause of the unhappiness, the parent may seem very upset or just a little upset.

Talking to your parent might help when he is unhappy.

We all have different ways of knowing when our parents are unhappy. Here is a list of common warning signals for kids to watch out for:

- eating a lot
- not talking
- going to sleep early
- not saying hi when they come home from work
- chain smoking
- ripping the room apart
- arguing with cashiers
- constantly cleaning things
- snapping at everyone
- ignoring your questions
- making fun of your friends
- beating up on the pets
- driving too fast
- yelling at other drivers and beeping the horn unnecessarily
- slamming doors
- staring blankly at the TV

Some of us have developed easy ways of telling when a parent is not happy. Elizabeth told us, "It is often very obvious when a parent is angry or in a bad mood. Some parents are quite frank and tell the child, 'I'm in a bad mood, so be careful.' Some parents simply imply that they're in a bad mood and expect their children to get the picture."

Tanya said, "I can tell if my parents are in a bad mood when they sit around and don't do anything productive, when they yell at me for no reason, when they mope around the house, and when they tell me they're in a bad mood."

If you find your parent in a bad mood, you can react in two ways. You can do what's easiest and best for you — don't talk to them, go to your room, and stay out of the way — or you can try to make them feel better. This involves doing anything they ask (especially lots of chores), being cheery and optimistic with them, and not losing your patience with them. It's a good idea not to ask them silly questions or bother them with little matters. You might do some nice things for them without being asked

— take the dog for a walk, bring them coffee in bed, make them some food, and take care of younger siblings. Some parents just need to be told to go to their room and lie down.

Kama described one helpful way children might react if their parents are in a bad mood. "When they come home," she said, "say hi in a cheerful way. Make sure you didn't leave a mess. After you say hi, go into your room for a while, until they get settled. Then come out and ask what is wrong and how was their day, but don't bug them. See if they want you to do anything and then just stay away from them until they're in a better mood."

If a parent is in a bad mood, the easiest way for them to let us know is to tell us bluntly. This does require a reasonable amount of tactfulness, which cannot always be expected from parents, especially when they are not very happy. Parents should think about what they are going to say to their child to let them know that they're in a bad mood. Maybe saying "I had a bad day at work and I'm very tired" (if this is the case) is best. They could also say, "I would appreciate it if you would be as quiet as possible and leave me alone. I'm in a bad mood, but it has nothing to do with you, so don't worry." It also helps if parents let you know when their condition has improved and their bad mood is over.

We've noticed that our parents are frequently in unpleasant moods at different times of the day or week. It's helpful for a child to notice when their parent is regularly grumpy and plan for this occasion. Caleb considers from 5:00 to 6:00, after his mother gets home from work, the "Danger Zone." Jesse thinks everyone in his family is in a bad mood at about 7:30 on Sunday nights, when another week of work and school are facing everyone. Ana's mom tends to hit her bad moods when she wakes up in the morning.

Find the time your parents are not happy and plan accordingly.

There have been times when our parents have been in bad moods and have handled them well. Tanya told us, "Once my stepmother had a really bad day at work and when she came home, she said, 'Tanya, I'm in a really bad mood, so just stay away from me.' This was good and helpful because I knew what to do and knew she was in a bad mood."

Josh and his brother once handled their mom's bad mood really well. He told us, "Once my mother came home from work very hassled and tired. We were used to this so we — my brother and I — had cleaned up the house before she got back. She was delighted."

Macy once did not handle her father's bad mood very well. She said, "One time this year when my dad was taking me to school, I got him really upset. He was already late for work and, right when we were about to leave, I decided to do some elaborate hairdo. This got him really burned up."

Once Gillian also didn't handle her parent's angry mood well, but she didn't know her mom was angry. She told us, "I had just gotten back from a friend's house and didn't know my parents had had a fight. I needed some help with math homework, so I went to my mother. She started to scream at me. I knew something had happened."

There are also times that you will notice your parent is in a good mood. It is important to notice and appreciate these moods and it is sometimes good to remember them when your parents are in bad moods. Mindy's mom is often in a good mood after dinner and also on Thursday nights because *Hill Street Blues* is on television. Andre's mom likes to cook, so dinnertime is a good time for her.

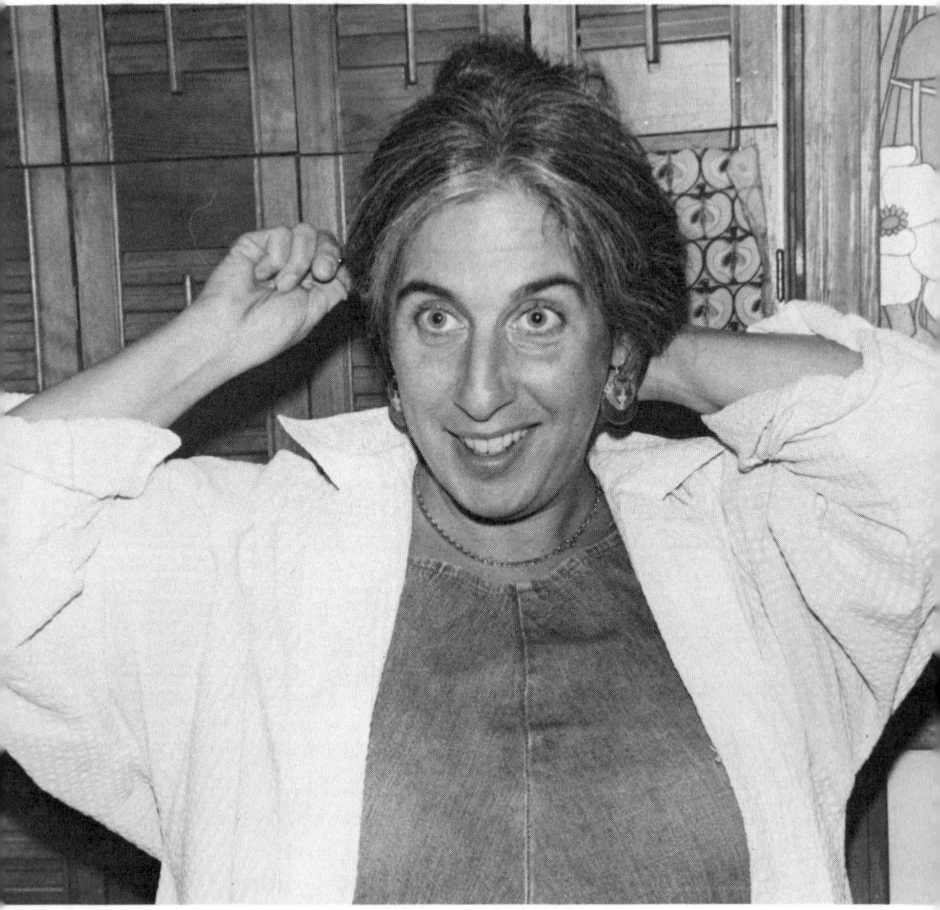

Caleb's mother is in a good mood in the morning.

Other times we've noticed some parents in good moods are all weekend, at the start of vacations (they're often in bad moods at the end of vacations), after they get a phone call from a friend or when they have a good day at work. Caleb's mom is in a good mood most mornings and wakes up energized and goes around the house being very cheery.

Some of the things we've noticed that parents do when they're in good moods are:

buy presents for kids
compliment kids
give you dinner choices
tickle kids
sing
walk funny
indulge kids
say strange things
use weird and affectionate names for kids like "pooder-role"
act nice to pets, even if they have misbehaved
joke or laugh hysterically
pretend they are someone else
be outrageous or silly
put on Jane Fonda records and exercise
move to radio music
make bad puns

When a parent is in a good mood, it's a good idea not to destroy it by being awful to them. However, it is also a good time to ask for favors and to bring up issues that are best discussed in a good mood. Kids have to make individual judgments about when is a good time to bring these things up with a parent. If you're not careful, a good mood can quickly turn into a bad mood.

Rules and Punishments

Most families have rules that people are expected to follow. Some of these rules are very clear and very obvious (such as, everyone has to clean up after themselves), and others are not very clear or obvious. Some families have rules that change with the parents' moods.

We think it's important for rules to be made and followed by both kids and parents. Although it sometimes seems that rules are silly and not at all useful, the purpose of rules is to help kids stay out of situations that they can't handle yet. Becca thinks her family has rules so that Becca and her brother will learn to take care of themselves. Elizabeth thinks that rules help to keep order in the household, and Stephen thinks that rules help teach kids a sense of responsibility. It seems obvious to us that families need rules just like society needs rules. As Josh said, "If it weren't for rules, people would be free to do anything they like at any time to anybody. Can you imagine a society in which killing or stealing weren't crimes?"

In some families the parents make all the rules; the kids have no say and, in fact, the rules are usually just there — they're not even explained to the kids. If a rule doesn't make sense, the kid isn't allowed to question it or argue against it. We don't think this is a good situation because children's opinions are not respected and they are forced to follow some rules that they might disagree with. It's probably easier for parents to make the rules themselves and force the kids to live by these rules, but it's not fair at all.

We feel that rules should be established with every family member present. They should all sit down and talk about the rules and try to reach some agreement. If necessary, a reasonable compromise should be made and both the parents and the children should be responsible for following the rules. Some rules could come from the parents and some rules could come from the kids.

Stephen thinks that families should keep a book of rules. He said, "Everyone in the family should think about things they have done recently that were not good for themselves, for someone else in the family, or for the family as a whole. They should write down rules about these things and keep them in a little book somewhere in the house. If something comes up that is not against one of the rules, yet it doesn't seem like a good thing for the person to do, they shouldn't get yelled at or punished. The family should talk about it and maybe write down a new rule in the rule book."

Many families have rules for the kids but not for the parents. In general, we feel that many rules should be used for every household member. Josh thinks that both parents and children should follow a rule like "take your boots off before walking through the front door," because even the parents can't avoid getting mud or snow on their boots. Of course, other rules shouldn't be applied to both the parent and the child. Kris said, "I'm not supposed to watch television in the daytime. Why should my mother have to follow this same rule?"

Talking to your parent about rules is important.

Sometimes we find ourselves in situations where there is a family rule that we don't like or that was helpful when we were younger but is no longer very helpful to us. In this case, Gillian thinks that the child should talk to his or her parents about it and ask to change the rule, giving very clear reasons. In most cases, the parents will listen, think about it, and be flexible about the rule. Kids should make sure to bring up this change of rule at the right time, after they've thought about it, come up with some good reasons to change the rule, and thought of a new rule to substitute for it. Kris thinks that if kids are in a situation where they want a rule changed, "they should break the rule, but pretend that you didn't mean to. Then tell your parent how you feel about the rule."

Part of dealing with rules involves dealing with punishments. This is often a big issue between parent and child because we sometimes have strong feelings about what kinds of punishments are okay and what kinds of punishments aren't. For example, we feel that hitting a child forcefully is *never* an acceptable punishment. As Elizabeth said, "Under no circumstance should a parent hit, slap, spank, thump, or abuse a child in any way for any reason. This could seriously injure the child, mentally as well as physically. I think this should be an illegal punishment, not to mention that it is cruel and mean. If parents can't find another way to express angry emotions, they should see someone about it."

Ana thinks that hitting a child is wrong and that "if you talk to the child, she will understand that she has done something wrong. If the child doesn't respond, then there are other punishments that can be used besides hitting."

Joachim also feels that any kind of physical punishment is wrong, "both because it hurts, and because it creates a love based on fear."

Kris feels that "slapping a kid and hitting them around like they were some kind of toy is really cruel." She thinks, however, "that one *light* spanking can be okay. For me, at least, when I got spanked it let out all of my anger. Afterward, I thought over what I'd done and usually I realized that it was wrong. Then my parents and I would make up."

We made a list of the most effective punishments for each of us:

TANYA: talking things out and guilt-tripping
JOSH: probably grounding, but it's never happened to me
GILLIAN: being sent to my room or yelled at
JOACHIM: taking away my allowance
JONATHAN: grounding
KRIS: being yelled at or not being allowed to have friends over
HEATHER: grounding
ELIZABETH: grounding and telephone restrictions
ANA: getting talked to and made to feel guilty

Sometimes punishments aren't really needed. Ana told us, "One day after school, I went to a friend's house when I was told not to go. I got in trouble. My mom told me why she didn't want me to go there and I felt really guilty. Now I understand why she feels this way and I even agree with her."

We like it when parents listen to us and consider our opinions about rules and punishments. Josh said, "For many years, my family has had a rule about no eating or drinking in the TV room. It was a good rule when I was young, but recently it has become a pain. So I asked my parents and they say it's okay for me to eat there, as long as my younger brother doesn't see."

Sometimes it's hard when you live in two different households and your parents have two sets of rules. It's hard to keep the rules straight and know how to act in each situation. Parents should be understanding of kids in these situations. It's also hard if you move from a situation with lots of rules to a situation with very few rules. Elizabeth's family always had very strict rules, but when she moved to Cambridge to live with her aunt, there was a great change. Her aunt wasn't very strict and Elizabeth found herself taking advantage of the situation. This ended quickly when Elizabeth's aunt learned how to say no.

We have good rules and bad rules that we've had to live with. The good rules some of us have in our households are:

TANYA: Clean up after yourself.
Do not play music too loudly.
If you are awake before other people, you have to be quiet.
Do not roughhouse in the house.
MINDY: Clean up my room.
Do homework with no argument.
Take care of the dog.
JOSH: Don't let your room become a serious fire hazard.
Don't eat messy foods anywhere but the kitchen.
Children can't light matches when a parent isn't around.
JOACHIM: No talking on the phone after 9:00 P.M.
Be home from school by 5:00 P.M.
JONATHAN: Do not beat on my sister.
Do not stay up after 10:00 on school nights.
Do not eat food that's intended for lunches.

We also talked about rules that are not good — even though some kids we know are expected to live by them. Tanya has friends who have to follow these unfair rules: no eating between meals; no phone calls after 6:00 P.M.; no music that parents don't like; no phone conversations over ten minutes.

Elizabeth knows a girl who has to live with these rules, which she thinks are ridiculous: no eating after 6:00 P.M.; no

Playing music too loudly will upset parents.

playing in the snow; no rock and roll (only gospel music); no friends may come over unless their mothers are good friends with her mother; no candy or soda; no television shows except the religious programs.

Some rules we have to live by that we don't like include not being able to have friends sleep over on week nights and not being able to watch television until after chores are done. Gillian has to answer the phone in her house because, as her parents put it, "it's always for Gillian."

The rules we like best are the rules with clear reasons behind them. Stephen told us, "I think my mother making me wear a helmet on my bicycle is a good rule because I don't really want to smash my skull apart. I think having to do jobs around the house is a good rule because otherwise the whole house would be a wreck. I think talking on the phone for only fifteen minutes at a time is a good rule because otherwise the phone would be tied up and nobody would be able to call. Acting in a civilized manner at all times is also fine."

Stephen also told us about some rules that he thinks are unfair. He said, "A friend of mine is always having to do schoolwork, chores, and more work during the summer vacation. I think this is an outrageous rule. He also invited another friend and me over for a slumber party and he and his little brother got into a fight (that his brother started) and, as punishment to him, the other kid and I got sent home."

We think that parents should have to suffer some kind of consequences if they break rules but, on a practical level, we don't think this will really happen. Sometimes it's enough if the parent simply confesses to the child. Tanya told us that her friend's family has a rule that if you play music too loudly, you aren't allowed to play your music for a week. When the girl's parents played their music too loudly, they were punished and didn't play their music for a week. We think this is a fair kind of situation, but most kids we know don't have parents punish themselves for breaking family rules.

PART III

Good Times We Have Had with Our Parents

The Importance of Having Fun Together

It's very easy for us to think of all the problems that we have with our parents, but we think it is also important to take some time to think about the good times. One of the major problems kids have with parents is that we don't make a conscious decision to do fun things together. This is often because parents and kids are so busy these days that no one has the time to plan activities that are simply good ways to spend time together. Kids are so busy with schoolwork and parents are so busy with their work that they usually don't have time for trips to the beach, special vacations, or playing sports together.

We think that it is important for parents and kids to make sure to spend some time together *each week* doing activities that are simply fun — not controversial or problem-causing. These could be activities that the parents do with all the kids or things that one parent and one child do together. The activity could involve anything from simply reading a book together and talking about it, taking a fun car ride, or seeing a movie together to going away on vacation, going out to eat, or spending a holiday or birthday together. We have noticed that often, unless someone thinks of it and plans the activity, weeks go by without us spending some good times together. Since we spend enough time arguing together and doing routine activities around our homes, we think it's important for both kids and parents to insist on spending some good times together.

One day in class, we made a list of all the fun things we could think of that some of us had experienced with our parent or parents. Not all of us enjoy each of the following activities, but here is a list of generally good things for parents and kids to do together:

Playing cards with your family can be fun.

see a movie
go skiing
go camping
play sports
swim
celebrate holidays
ride bikes
see a car race
shop for presents
visit a zoo
go out to eat
go sailing
run or watch a marathon
have a picnic
go to the horse races
get haircuts together
go to a concert
visit relatives
play video games
read aloud to each other
ride horses
play with pets
go to the Olympics
play board games
visit a carnival
see the Ice Capades
have a party
have supper together
go on a vacation
go trick-or-treating
see a circus
paint the house
have a barbecue
go sightseeing
go for a drive
watch a TV show
celebrate a birthday
visit a museum
go bowling
call out for Chinese food
go to an arcade
go fishing
cook a meal together
play miniature golf

This is a long list, so if you are looking for a way to have fun with your parents, look it over and suggest a few activities they might enjoy. You might also think of some activities that aren't on the list.

Keep in mind that all these activities can turn into bad times if you are not careful. Things like bad weather, bad moods, and disagreements about food or money can cause problems even if you are planning a fun event together.

In this section we look at some of the good times we have had with our parents and we suggest ways in which other kids and parents can enjoy these activities. Before you can really participate in these activities and enjoy them, however, you have to decide that you want to spend time together and realize that even when parents and children do things together that don't result in a major accomplishment (like building a model or repairing an appliance), they can be building their relationship and enjoying each other's company. Especially for young children, fun time together with parents is very important. As we get older, we want to spend more fun time with friends our own age, but if we have established a pattern of spending time with our parents, we think it will continue into our teenage years.

Vacations

It's fun to go away on vacations because there are many things you can do as a family while you are away. For the kids, it's a good way to learn about a new place or some new things, and for the parents, it's a good excuse for taking time off. Everyone comes back with some good memories, too. Some vacations can be very relaxing and some can be very active — especially if you want to see something in particular. If you live in the city all the time, vacations are a good time to get to the country. We also enjoy going on vacation and visiting relatives we like.

For everybody's sake, vacations should be planned, in order to prevent some of the problems that might arise. We don't encourage families to plan every minute of the vacation, but some general discussion well ahead of time is helpful in preventing parents from not letting the kids do anything that they like and in avoiding a lot of disagreements on the trip about places to go and things to do.

Vacations can sometimes cause kids to get into embarrassing situations. Once, when Nat and his folks went on a vacation in Nevada, his folks were swimming without their clothes on and the police came and caught them. Nat was very embarrassed. Macy had a similar situation because her parents sometimes end up playing "typical tourists" on vacation. When they went to Aqua World in Florida, her parents insisted Macy pose for a picture next to a big plastic shark. Macy had no choice about this and felt stupid standing next to this fake fish.

One of the biggest problems that can ruin a vacation is boredom. The whole purpose of vacation, it seems to us, is to have fun and do some exciting activities, and if kids' interests aren't included as a part of the vacation plan, they might as well stay home and watch television. We want parents and kids to plan vacations together and compromise whenever needed so that everyone is able to have a good time. We recommend that the family plan some time together doing things that everyone likes, some time when the kids have to do things that only the parents really want to do, and some time when the parents have to do things that the kids want to do.

Most of us have had good experiences with vacations and have found them a way to enjoy our parents and share some time together without a great deal of arguing or fighting. Caleb went to Africa with his dad and enjoyed seeing new places, especially the animals and the city of Nairobi. They went up in a hot air balloon and toured the countryside. This was when Caleb was eleven years old.

Tanya and her father and stepmother went to Bermuda and visited Sea World, lots of museums, and went sightseeing in the Crystal Caves. Tanya thought this was a good vacation where they had lots of fun and kept busy all the time.

Vacations don't have to be far away from home and, in fact, can be single-day or weekend trips. Ana and her mother and her sister went to visit the famous mansions in Newport, Rhode Island, just a few hours from Boston. Ana had a good time and remembered that, in one of the big mansions, they walked through it and got lost together and had a difficult time finding their way out. This was a fun thing to do with a parent.

Going Out to Eat

Most of us like to go out to eat with our parents. Going out to eat can be a fun activity for kids and parents because it's good to get out of the house and no one has to set the table and wash the dishes — someone else waits on you. You can have the chance to eat different kinds of food and, usually, you don't have to order what you don't want to eat. This is often a chance for parents to relax and have a good time, and most of us think that our parents usually will not fight in a restaurant, which is a little different than mealtime at home.

Problems can arise, however, when you're at a restaurant with your parents. One time, David was embarrassed when his baby brother spilled his milk on a neighboring table. Some of us have had similar problems when we have spilled things by accident and our parents have gotten overly upset. We've also been embarrassed when the food was not to someone's liking and our parents made a big scene about it and complained to the manager.

Food fights can also be a problem, because they tend to upset parents a lot (probably because they get embarrassed that their kids are acting like kids and not like nice adults). If there's been a problem with food fights in the past, it's a good idea for parents to talk to kids about it ahead of time and make some rules. When a very small child throws food, someone should take away the food until they calm down.

We recommend that people — especially kids — read the menu for the restaurant before they settle into their seats. Make sure that you like at least one food offered. If you are served your food and you don't like it, nothing can really be done about it. But we urge you not to make a big fuss; simply make sure you don't order that food the next time you're in the restaurant. Picky eaters should try to not be very picky when they're in restaurants and use it as an opportunity to try new foods.

Some kids like to order the most expensive thing on the menu. Some parents don't mind this, but some do. Sometimes people spend more money than they plan to spend when they go out for a meal and occasionally they spend more money then they have brought with them. We recommend that kids ask the parents before ordering the most expensive entrée and that families sometimes go to less expensive restaurants where money doesn't have to be a big consideration.

Another problem that can arise is that you might be waited on by an obnoxious waiter or waitress. You could let this ruin your meal or you could spend the whole meal talking about that person with your parents. We generally try to pay no attention to these people and not let them ruin our meal. If you get an obnoxious waiter or waitress, we suggest that you give them less of a tip at the end of the meal.

We've all had some good experiences going out to eat with our parents. Ana once went to a French restaurant with her mother, who suggested that Ana try the chocolate mousse for dessert. She ordered it, took a big bite, and then realized there was a lot of alcohol in it! It gave Ana a funny feeling.

Tanya and her father and stepmother went out to eat at Quincy Market, a fancy shopping area in downtown Boston. Tanya's stepmother announced to everyone that it was Tanya's sixth birthday and then had a cake brought out and the whole place sang happy birthday. This was very funny because, in fact, Tanya was twelve years old.

Sports and Games

Many of us enjoy playing games and sports with our parents. Sports are good for exercise, and playing a sport with your parent can improve your skills and make you a better player when you play with your friends. For the parents, sports and games can be fun because lots of parents don't get enough exercise and sometimes playing games with their kids brings back memories of their own childhood. Both boys and girls like playing sports and games with parents.

Of course, sports can also cause problems between a parent and a child. Some kids are forced to play sports that they don't enjoy. This is no fun at all. Some parents are overprotective, and spend the whole time telling the kids to be careful, and not play too rough, instead of trusting us to be careful on our own. Also, sometimes parents and kids disagree on rules.

We suggest that you talk about sports and games with your parents before you play them together — not a long time in advance, but just before you play. The activity chosen should be one that both the child and the parent enjoy and the rules should be set in advance, with both sides compromising where necessary.

Sometimes funny things happen when you're involved

in sports with your parent. Tanya and her dad were skiing down a difficult slope once and she was a little scared. Her father tried to calm her down and said, "Here's how to do it properly." Then he fell down.

Heather's mom is not really into sports, but last year decided that she would begin to go swimming regularly with Heather. She would get a little nervous about some of Heather's diving, mainly because Heather wasn't really experienced in diving and neither was her mother. They talked about it and worked things out so they could still go swimming together.

Gillian's dad got the idea that it would be fun for the whole family to go swimming together one time at an indoor pool in Cambridge. Gillian remembers this as a very special, fun family outing.

Watching sports can also be a fun thing to do with your parents — going to a football or basketball game or watching a tennis match. For kids or parents that don't like to exercise a lot, this can be a relaxing way to enjoy sports together as a family.

Going to the Movies

Movies are fun for both parents and kids. They give a family an interesting time away from the home, and they give you something to discuss that you are not so personally involved in. We like the fact that parents almost always pay for the movies, too.

Choosing a movie to see may be difficult, especially if the kid wants to see a movie very badly and the parents don't want to see it at all. We urge everyone to be open to new ideas when they're considering a movie to see. Nat, for example, wanted to see *Blade Runner* and kept bothering his father to go see it. Finally, after a lot of nagging, his father reluctantly agreed, even though he really doesn't like science fiction movies. His father ended up liking the movie.

Ana and her mother go to the movies together regularly. They alternate on who chooses the movie. This seems to work out fine.

Food can become an issue when you go to a movie: kids not being allowed to get the candy they want, pigging out on too much popcorn and feeling sick, spending too much money. We recommend that parents and kids set rules together about the food they eat at movies. Some of us bring our own food into the movies, mainly because movie theaters charge such high prices for candy these days.

It's sometimes hard to go to the movies as a family because siblings are different ages, have different interests, sometimes fight and make noise, and are generally hyper. The parent has to play a disciplining role in this case, which we bet is not a good way for them to enjoy the movie. We think that the best thing for parents to do is to use subtle threats with their kids if they are not behaving in the movie. This works with us.

Whether or not a kid should be allowed to go to an R-rated movie is a big issue in families, especially when the kids get to be our ages — around eleven to fourteen. This is something that parents and kids will have to discuss and decide upon together, but the parents really seem to have the upper hand in this decision because, unless you're lucky, kids can't get into these movies without an adult. Once you get into an R-rated movie, it can sometimes be a little embarrassing. Ana didn't understand a "dirty" joke in one of these movies and her mom explained it to her — loud enough so everyone in the theater could hear. Ana sank down under her seat in embarrassment.

Andre had a similar experience. He saw the movie *The Toy* in which there was a character named Master Bates. Andre laughed at the name a lot but his mother got mad at him and said, "I don't think that's funny. It's disgusting!" We generally find it uncomfortable when you laugh at something in a movie that has to do with sex and then your parents have a long talk with you after, explaining what the joke was about and telling you why it wasn't funny.

Parents and kids can use movies to discuss controversial issues or just to talk about something and share their views on it. Sometimes, however, fights occur, or people argue their point of view and don't listen to the other side. Jonathan and his mother had a long argument about what the meaning of the movie *E.T.* was. One kid we know went to a really terrible movie, but the parent and the kid both hated it and were able to talk about the movie's faults afterward. This was a good experience after all. One kid we know went to a movie he hated, but because his parent liked it a lot, he didn't say anything. He just pretended to like the movie and felt bad about it.

Going to the Beach

The beach is a good place for parents and kids to go when the weather is nice. A trip to the beach can be a relaxing, day-long outing for the family and, for families living in the city, a good way to get into the country. Also the family can enjoy certain sports, such as swimming and waterskiing.

The beach, however, can cause a lot of problems — such as getting sunburned, little kids getting lost, and getting sand in your lunch — and conflicts — such as parents not letting kids swim without strict supervision (overprotective parent) or swim far enough out in the water to enjoy themselves. Sometimes parents don't want to stay at the beach long enough, so kids are not given enough time to have fun.

We think that, the night before a trip to the beach, families should plan how much time they will spend there. They should discuss the schedule, the rules, and what they will do, keeping an open mind and compromising whenever necessary. We also think that both kids and parents should take responsibility for doing some of the work in preparation for the trip, and that kids should be sure to bring equipment and games to keep them interested, in case they begin to get bored.

All of us have some good memories of going to the beach with our parents. Kristin remembers how playful her dad is on the beach and how he would twirl her around and go swimming with her. Jesse remembers a time he went to Cape Cod with his father who caught a thirty-pound, three-foot-long bass. Jesse carried the fish up a hill for his father and, because he was ten years old at the time and the fish was almost as big as he was, everyone seemed impressed.

Joachim went with his father and stepmother to the beach in South Carolina and enjoyed going on beach walks together and going fishing. Nat remembers learning how to swim from his father and a friend of the family and thinks this is a good thing that parents and kids can do together.

We feel angry when parents take us to the beach and don't go into the water, especially if there are no other kids around to play with in the water. It's boring for us and we want them to do more than just get a tan. Some of the reasons we've noticed that some parents don't go in the water are that they're too tired, the water's too cold, they are too busy people-watching, or that they are too busy getting a tan.

If your parents are planning on staying out of the water, they should encourage you to bring a friend to the beach. They should at least go down to the water and watch you swim and talk with you a little. Be careful not to splash them, even if you're doing it as a joke. A lot of parents get angry about this.

Holidays

Holidays are traditionally times when kids and parents are together and they can be fun for both the children and the adults involved. Holidays can be occasions for everyone to relax and ignore work and school, and if you are religious or care about the meaning of a particular holiday, they can be deeper personal experiences. They're also often times when people eat a lot of good food and give each other presents — two things most kids like a lot.

We all have some special family traditions that go along with holidays. David enjoys helping his aunt bake bagels for many of the Jewish holidays. John's mother and father make doughnuts with him on Christmas Eve. Ana enjoys reading the instructions on her family's assemble-it-yourself Christmas tree on Christmas Eve and trying to figure out how to put it together.

For Christmas, Macy and her mom make rice pudding and hide almonds inside the pudding; whoever finds the almonds gets good luck. Matt enjoys Halloween because he and his mother bake pumpkin seeds and then eat

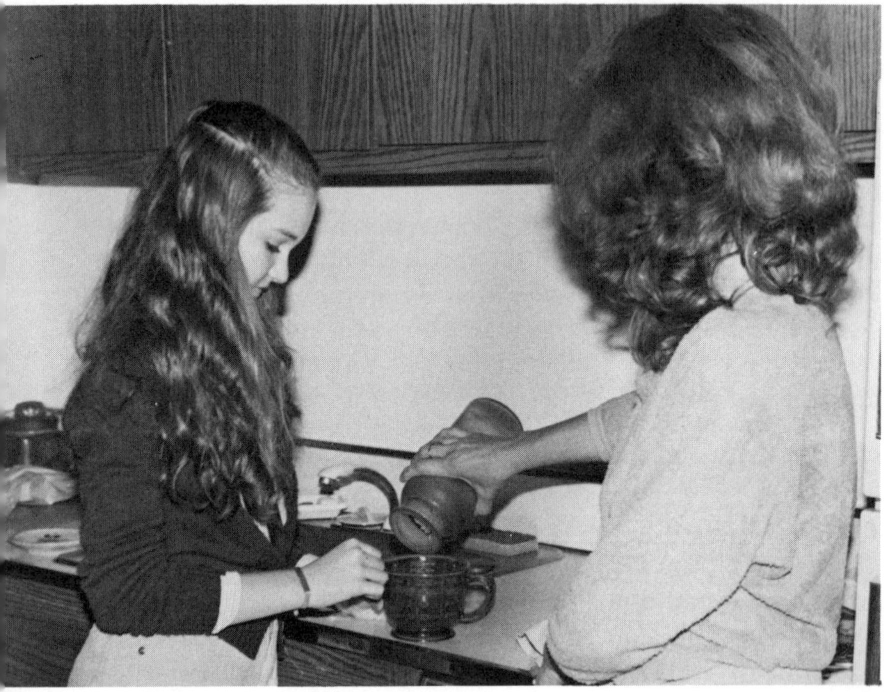

Macy and her mother prepare holiday rice pudding.

them. Kris enjoys Easter because her mother steals everyone's jellybeans.

Even though holidays are basically fun, problems can arise — problems with sibling rivalry or relatives that don't get along or don't speak to each other at all. On gift-giving holidays, kids sometimes receive gifts that they don't like or don't need and don't receive some of the gifts that they really want. You might get a gift you don't like from a relative who is sitting right next to you, so you have to lie and pretend you like it just to be polite and not hurt their feelings.

Some of us have problems because our parents feel the religious aspects of holidays are important and we don't. They force us to go to church or synagogue, which we feel is useless and unfair. And those of us who are Jewish and don't celebrate Christmas sometimes feel left out of the excitement.

It is probably a good idea for families to plan holidays together and develop their own traditions. We think that there are some very special things that parents and kids can do around the holidays and that, unless children have input into how the family celebrates the day, they might feel left out and end up having a mediocre day.

Birthdays and Parties

Kids like birthdays because they enjoy the feeling of togetherness that usually takes place, receiving gifts, growing up, and the excitement that occurs. Birthdays are nice times for the whole family to get together and focus their attention on the person celebrating the birthday.

Birthdays can be difficult when a kid doesn't live with both parents but wants to be with them both. (This is true for holidays, also.) Some families we know solve this problem by having both parents put their differences aside and get together on the kid's birthday or the holiday and trying just to have a nice day focused on the kid. Other kids we know spend part of the day with each parent.

Birthdays sometimes bring up problems for kids and parents. Sometimes we get gifts that we don't like and sometimes we give gifts that someone doesn't want. It's very hard to figure out a present to get for your father and mother. We've gotten helpful ideas from older siblings or from adult friends of the family. It's embarrassing to forget to buy someone a present on their birthday and it's helpful if kids can be reminded when special occasions like this are coming up.

Parties can be fun for kids, but sometimes they can be unenjoyable. Jesse once had a party at McDonald's and it was horrible because it was embarrassing when they sang happy birthday to him in public and, anyway, the cake tasted like toothpaste.

One kid we know had a party that was a lot of fun because there was a big scavenger hunt organized by the parents, which turned out to be great.

Families have parties for reasons other than birthdays, too. Kids can have fun parties just to bring their friends together, parents often have parties for their friends, and sometimes parents and the kids invite friends to a joint party. Parties are good ways for parents to get to know some of the kid's friends; for kids to meet their parents' friends; for kids and parents to enjoy games together; and for everyone to listen to music, eat a lot, and have a good time.

We've noticed a lot of problems that can come up when kids have parties. Rules really need to be discussed and agreed on ahead of time to avoid some of these problems. It really is the job of both the parents and the kids to make sure these rules are followed. Problems can arise for many reasons, including: kids bringing drugs or alcohol to the party, the music being played too loudly, too much noise being made, or if food fights occur. Once you get to be a teenager, parents become concerned if socializing and any kind of "sexual activity" takes place. At parents' parties problems arise because some parents scream and yell and get drunk and a lot of tensions can come up. Another problem related to parties is that a lot of kids and parents disagree on fashions and on what kind of clothing is suitable to wear.

Tanya had a good experience with a party that she had at her dad's house. Tanya and her stepmother agreed ahead of time that if something went wrong, Tanya would handle it. Clear limits were set and nobody freaked out when the problems came up. Tanya handled things as agreed. Her parents liked most of her friends and now they ask her, "When are you going to have another party?"

Heather remembers her tenth birthday party as a good experience. She was living in a big house and invited forty kids, expecting about twenty to show up. A lot more people came than she expected. Heather and her mother quickly decided on the way they would handle the situation. Heather told us, "We decided that if something happened that my mother disapproved of a little bit but it didn't really cause harm, we'd let it go. I was expected to handle the problems that came up." Heather had a fun time at the party and so did her mother. Only small problems came up and Heather handled them. Most of all, Heather liked that her friends saw her mother in a non-stressful situation and was glad that her friends liked her mom.

Riding in the Car

Most of us enjoy riding in the car with our parents. Except on very long boring trips, car rides can give a kid a chance to see a lot of new places and spend time with the parent in a relaxed way. It is also fun to listen to the radio, play car games, and stop for food.

Some of the most frequent problems that come up with car rides involve how loud the music should be and which radio station should be listened to, whether seat belts are on, if the kids are making too much noise, bathroom stops, asking "are we there yet?" too frequently, tension caused by traffic jams, parent driving too fast or too slow for the kid, child criticizing the parent's driving, whether the windows should be opened, who sits where, and the parent smoking and the kid complaining.

These sound like a lot of problems to arise in a simple car ride but we do know that they come up frequently. We think that if parents and kids want car rides to be pleasant, they ought to establish some rules together. Some of the things we've heard about that help are:

kids respecting the parents' need for peace and quiet while they are driving
parents not being so strict about the radio
kids not asking a lot of questions
everyone keeping the conversation civilized
everyone compromising when conflicts come up
going to the bathroom before you leave
thinking of fun things to do in the car
parents driving within the speed limit

Some of the good things to do when you are on a ride with your parents are discuss school or work, or listen to music that you both like. Kama told us, "I save a lot of things to talk about with my mother for when we are in the car." We think this is a good idea. John told us, "I like car games because they help to combat the boredom. Paying the tolls is also fun." It can be fun to bring snacks in the car, also.

Some of the families we know have rules about the radio. One idea is to compromise on a station both the kid and the parent like, even if it is not the favorite station of either. Another thing that you can do is to listen to one station for a half an hour and then the other person gets to listen to their station.

Since some kids spend a lot of time with their parents in a car, it is important to find a way to make this a good time together. A little bit of thought and planning should help any family with car rides.

PART IV

The Problems and Rewards of Living in Different Kinds of Families

Most of this book was written in a way that doesn't take into account the kind of family that a child lives in. This is because we believe that most kids and parents have to deal with similar issues, whether they live in a nuclear family or a divorced family, whether they have parents who work or a mother who stays home with them all the time. No matter what family situation you are in, you will find that you need to work out some issues with your parents — things like bedtimes, allowance, vacations, and rules.

When we talked as a group about our families, we realized that we come from all kinds of families. Some of us live with our two original parents, others with a single parent. Some of us have divorced parents and commute back and forth between them, and others of us very rarely (even never) see one of our parents. Some of us live in a household with other adults and kids who are not even related to us, and some of us live with adults who aren't our original parents — such as an aunt or grandparent. Today kids live in many, many family forms and we recognize that each form has special problems and special joys.

In this section, we discuss over a dozen kinds of families that are most common in our school and in America today.

We hope to explain what it is like to live in different kinds of families and to help kids see the best ways to relate to their parents in these families.

Living in a Nuclear Family

The "classic" nuclear family consists of a mother who stays home and bakes brownies, a father who is the breadwinner of the family and goes to work each day, and 2.5 "perfect" kids. But the classic nuclear family doesn't exist too often today.

In the modern nuclear family, the children still live with both parents — there has been no divorce or death in the family — but the mother might work outside the home and there might be fewer than 2.5 kids. Often there is a dog or a cat involved as well. The nuclear family is still very common and lots of kids live in this situation.

Kristin likes living in a nuclear family, mainly because she never has lived any other way. Jake lives in a nuclear family too and he likes having everyone in his family live together in the same home. Gillian and Jonathan also live in nuclear families and they are happy with their situations.

One of the best parts of living in a nuclear family is that you don't have to deal with a divorce or with custody situations that involve not seeing very much of one of your parents. In a nuclear family you always have another parent to go to if one is mad at you or in a bad mood. It is also nice that you can be close to both of your parents throughout your childhood instead of having only one parent who has to take on all the responsibilities.

Although most people think of the nuclear family as the

"ideal" situation, there are still problems with this form of family. In most nuclear families we know, there are fights between the two parents, and many of the kids spend a lot of time being afraid that these fights mean that their parents are going to be divorced, which they think means their lives will be ruined. In nuclear families, the parents tend to agree on issues related to the kids and you frequently find yourself in situations where the argument becomes two against one — and the one is you. It is also kind of easy for parents to slip into very traditional roles in a nuclear family and you might find that your mother becomes frustrated with the typical role of mother (cleaning, baking cookies, visiting school) and your father isn't very open to changes.

We advise kids who live in a nuclear family not to spend a lot of time worrying about divorce or death. There's nothing you can do about the situation if it happens and you should realize that many kids live in divorced situations and single-parent families and have very nice lives. It also defeats one of the benefits of life in a nuclear family — that you are supposedly stable and secure — if all your time is spent worrying about whether the family will always stay together.

Dotty, a girl in our class, often seems in total bliss living in a nuclear family. In science class once, she made a little clay pot with a rainbow on it and said, "Because it's so colorful and happy, it reminds me of my family." Dotty lives with her parents and her older brother, Chip.

Kristin tells us, "I'm glad I live in a nuclear family and I don't have to go through divorce like some of my friends. That seems like a pretty rotten experience for them."

It is important for kids who live in nuclear families to realize that other family forms are fine ways of living and not to be uppity about their situation. Sometimes it's easy to assume every kid lives with a mother and father, and you can make an embarrassing mistake by getting surprised or shocked when you find that a friend doesn't live in this way. If this happens to you, keep in mind that everyone is human and makes mistakes and try to avoid the same mistake the next time.

Being Part of an Extended Family

Several of us have lived part of our lives in what is called an extended family. This means we've lived with our biological parent or parents, as well as our brothers or sisters, and also lived with another relative — like an aunt, uncle, grandparent, or cousin.

A long time ago, most kids lived in extended families. Their mother and father got married and still lived with one of their own parents. The children were brought up in a large family with a lot of contact with grandparents (even great-grandparents), aunts, uncles, and cousins. Nowadays, it is less common, but it's still a family situation many kids experience.

These days kids find themselves living in an extended family for a wide variety of reasons. Sometimes the parents divorce and the mother and the children go to live with the mother's parents for a while. Sometimes an extended family occurs because it is a way to save money and to have more adults available to stay with the kids and take them places. It's almost like living in a commune, except these people are actually your relatives.

Heather and her mom lived with her grandparents for a few months. She told us about some of the positive aspects: "There is always someone around and these extra people in your life might be good cooks and, if they drive, might be able to give you rides to places you want to go. Living in an extended family also cuts down on the amount of housework given to any one person."

She also told us about some of the negative things that kids should look out for: "You have to get used to a new way of life, such as new rules, especially if you and one or both of your parents are moving into someone else's home. You also might not get along with your relatives well enough to really live with them."

We like the fact that life in an extended family often means getting to know other relatives well and learning how to live with a lot of people. We are concerned, though, that kids get very attached to new people when they live in an extended family and then the parents might decide to move out and be a family by themselves again. This can cause troubles. There are also problems with who gets to set the rules and who is in charge of the kids. Sometimes when a mother moves in with her parents, she gets into fights with her parents about how to raise the child. The child can feel caught in the middle of this situation.

Kate ended up living in an extended family through a gradual change in her family's living situation. She was living with her mother and sister, but her mother went to school all day and Kate's grandmother baby-sat for the kids. As time went by, it turned out the grandmother was spending more and more time with the children, till they were all living together and Kate's mom was working most of the time. The fact that this happened gradually made it a comfortable situation and, eventually, Kate didn't want to leave this living arrangement.

Heather told us a story about how living in an extended family can be fun and helpful to kids. One morning,

Heather missed the bus and was late for a student council meeting at school. She was in tears because her grandmother had told her that if she missed the bus she wouldn't drive her to school. When Heather's grandfather found her crying and heard the whole story, he politely told her grandmother that he disagreed with her and drove Heather to school. On the way, he told Heather how this used to happen to her mother. Heather felt close to her grandfather and knew that he was on her side.

The other good thing about being in an extended family is that you sometimes get to live with people who are older than those many kids get to know. Living with a grandparent can be fun and interesting and might take some of the mystery out of old people for you. This could make it a lot easier to deal with growing up yourself and could also make you less afraid of dealing with elders in general.

Never Knowing One of Your Parents

Some kids are raised entirely by one of their parents and never see their other parent. This usually happens when parents are divorced when the child is very young and one parent gets custody of the child. If you never know one of your parents it could mean that he or she doesn't care about you or has left town and now lives very far away. This is a rough situation on a child, but it happens to many children these days.

Joy lives with her mother and has never seen her father. She really likes living with her mother and they get along very well. They share a lot of things, which makes them very close. Joy is curious about her father, but her mother never really discusses him. Sometimes, her mother asks if Joy misses her father. Joy said that she finds out things about her father by asking her grandparents. They tell Joy stories. Joy finds it interesting and fun to look at pictures of her father and to talk about him. She wants to know more and is very curious about him.

Some kids we know in similar situations feel very angry at the missing parent for not being there and they wonder why he or she isn't with them. In most of the situations we know about, the father is the absent parent and we wonder how fathers could just leave their child and not keep in touch. Some of us feel that we are missing something if we only have one parent. Ana feels that, by not having a father around, she misses out on some of the things kids generally do with their fathers.

We don't have any answers to the questions kids have about how parents could leave children and never see them. We can't imagine doing this ourselves, but we think that some parents must feel that the child is better off without them, or for some reason, it is a legal part of the custody arrangement after the divorce. We wish that this wouldn't happen, because the child is left to wonder and get paranoid about it.

Living with a Guardian

A guardian is an adult who takes responsibility for a child's care when the parent can no longer be responsible. Someone lives with a guardian when their parents are dead, their parents don't want them, it's more convenient to live with someone else, or the parents are away on a trip. Sometimes you might live with a guardian as a temporary situation when your parents are getting readjusted to new situations or are moving or separating. Foster care involves having special guardians for a while until your parent or parents are ready to take care of you again. The guardian's job is to make sure you are fed, clothed and cared for, and to make sure you stay out of trouble. Some guardians are very warm and nice and might have more time for you than your parents did, and others might just be people who are providing for you but don't really do a lot of parenting.

Elizabeth lives with her aunt in Cambridge, Massachusetts. Until she was eleven, she lived with her parents in Danville, Virginia. It was very hard to live in that situation because there were a lot of changes going on, so Elizabeth moved up to Cambridge and lived with her Aunt Sally.

Over the past three years, Elizabeth and her Aunt Sally have grown very close. Elizabeth still sees her parents very often, but she enjoys living with her aunt. Elizabeth told us, "The biggest disadvantage of this situation is that there are times I want to see my parents, brother, or sisters, and I can't. My way of solving this problem is by calling them when I really miss them."

Elizabeth also told us, "Some people might think that I would grow further apart from my parents and closer to my aunt, but actually I've grown a lot closer to my parents and my aunt."

Some of the advantages we see in living with a guardian are that you can get out of a stressful family situation and into a happier, more stable home. You might find that your guardian or foster parent has children your age that you can play with, and you might find that there are a lot of things that you like about your new home, neighborhood, or school. You may meet a lot of new people, and have the opportunity to make new friends.

The disadvantages are obvious: not seeing your parents enough; being given too many responsibilities by people who don't know what you are used to doing; and having to adjust to a new home, new friends, and a new school.

If you find yourself in a situation where you have to deal with guardians, we recommend that you treat them like parents and communicate honestly with them. Let them know what is going on in your head and be sure to tell them when things are going badly for you. You should let them know that some of their rules might be new and hard for you, but you should try to find a way to follow all the rules that make sense, and change the rules that you disagree with. If you find yourself in a situation with a guardian for just a few weeks, we recommend that you don't make a big deal about the problems you have with them and just try to make the time a pleasant, relaxing kind of vacation. The odds are that you have family crises and problems to deal with during this time and your major energy should go into sorting out that situation.

Being Part of a Stepfamily

A stepfamily means living with one of your original, or biological, parents and a stepmother or stepfather, and sometimes stepbrothers and -sisters or half-brothers or half-sisters (brothers or sisters who are the sons or daughters of your mother or father and a stepparent). This sounds complicated, but these situations are coming up for more and more kids all the time.

Many of us live in stepfamilies. David told us, "My situation is that I live with my mother and my stepfather. I like him because he is nice to me. For instance, he will help me with my math homework when I get stuck. However, he kind of influences my mother in an argument, sometimes, and this bothers me."

Mike lives part-time in a single-parent family with his mother, and part-time in a stepfamily with his father, his father's wife, and his two-year-old half-sister. Kate lives with her mother, her stepfather, and her sister. Tanya lives part-time with her mother, and part-time with her father and her stepmother.

Jesse lives part-time with his father and stepmother, Stephanie, and part-time with his mother. Stephanie is going to have a baby and Jesse isn't sure how to react to this. He told us that he likes having another adult around his father's house, although "sometimes she butts in when I don't think she should." He deals with this situation by confronting her when it comes up and they always work things out.

In general, most of us like our stepparents and most of us like the other children we live with in our stepfamilies. We are happy when a divorced parent meets someone they like, even though we sometimes feel jealous and hurt about it because it makes us realize that our two real parents aren't going to get back together.

One of the good things about living in a stepfamily is that you could get siblings that you like, particularly a brother or sister who is your age or older. You might be able to trust your stepparent and talk to him or her in a different way than you talk to your biological parent. You also might find that your parent is happier and more settled now that he or she has another adult to share life with.

Problems can also come up. It is a very bad situation if you find that you don't like your stepparent at all. You might also find that your stepfather or stepmother starts to act like they are your real parent and tries to discipline you or impose new and strange rules on you. This will have to be talked about as an entire family. We don't like it when we see the stepparent influencing our parent's opinion on an issue or argument in a new way and we generally feel that it is the stepparent's responsibility to make sure that things do not change dramatically just because they marry your mother or father.

There's not a lot you can do if you don't like your stepparent. You should try to be polite and see their good qualities. You should realize that it is most important that your parent likes this person and that you find a way to accept them into the family. You'll probably go through a range of feelings toward a stepparent in the first few years you live with them, and you shouldn't lock yourself into one opinion or attitude.

Stepparents should never try to take the place of your other parent, even if the parent has died. Your original parents are special and that situation cannot be changed. It is also important that stepparents not judge the other parent or try to win you away from them. If you develop a really good relationship with a stepparent, you might begin to consider them a third parent. However, this cannot take away from your original parents' roles in your life.

Dealing with Adoption

Some children are adopted or have a brother or sister who is adopted. Being adopted means that your parents are not your biological parents. An adopted child has biological parents who, for some reason, could not continue to be their guardian parents throughout life. Therefore, they put the child up for adoption. This usually means that they realized they couldn't provide the child with a good home and a nice life and wanted to make sure the child did have a good life.

Susanna, a girl who was in our class last year, was adopted when she was six weeks old. She considers her adopted mother and father to be her parents and, even though they have now divorced, she still sees them both. Susanna was told about being adopted when she was about seven years old. She thinks that if she was told about this when she was younger, she would not have understood what it meant. Susanna told us her reaction when she learned she was adopted: "I was kind of shocked. I wasn't mad or sad, just kind of shocked."

When Susanna was eight years old, a letter came from the adoption agency that took care of finding her a home. The letter asked her parents to send in Susanna's name and some information about how she felt about the adoption. After they sent that in, they received a reply letter, telling them Susanna's mother's name and a little bit about her. They didn't tell Susanna anything about her father.

Susanna told us that she has never really given serious thought to finding her biological mother. She says that she sometimes has wondered about what her biological mother looks like and where she is, but that she would never want to leave her current home to live with her biological mother.

We also asked Susanna if she would ever consider adopting a child herself when she grew up. She said that she might, and that it would be nice to adopt a baby, but that older kids need to be adopted more. Susanna thinks this might be because people think the older kids have problems because they have moved around from family to family and haven't had a permanent home.

If you are adopted, you might be embarrassed to tell your friends about it. This is your right, and you should only tell the people you feel comfortable telling. But we think that adoption is not a good reason to be embarrassed and it really isn't such a big deal. The big problems that we imagine some kids having with their adopted family are wishing that they were with their biological parents every time they have a fight with their current parents, wondering what their biological parents look like, and dealing with the mysteries that come with being adopted. It's also a little difficult to wonder why you were put up for adoption and it's easy for adopted kids to feel unloved and unwanted. We think it's better to think that your biological parents probably loved you a lot and were either too young to be good parents or just didn't have the money or the skills to be good parents, but loved you enough to find you a good home.

Enjoying Communal Living

Another form of family some kids we know live in is a commune. This is usually a big house where several different families live together and share meals, chores, and living expenses. Most kids in this situation still live with one or both of their parents, but they live with other adults and other children as well. Sometimes two families live together — especially two single-parent families — and share responsibilities and expenses. One girl we knew lived with her mother and another mother and daughter. It worked out well and they became very good friends.

Jamey has had the experience of living in a commune. She told us: "I was only three years old when we moved into the commune. We lived there for two years. I liked it a lot, because there were other kids living in the same building as me and we were friends.

"There was sort of a day-care center within the commune, where one of the members would stay with all the children while the parents worked. I'm sure that this was nice for the parents, because they didn't have to pay for child care. The kids liked it too, because we would play games and it was fun being with other little kids.

"One thing I didn't like about the commune I lived in was that, if you didn't like someone, you couldn't very well avoid them because they live in the same house with you."

We think that the big problem with communal living is understanding which adults have the right to act like your parent. Sometimes you might resent these adults telling you what to do. Most communes we've heard about are pretty open places and the adults tend to be pretty nice to kids, so this isn't necessarily that big a problem. It's important to maintain good communication with your own parent and be sure that if there are problems between you and other adults you get the help and support you need.

Communal life isn't for everyone, but for kids, there are a lot of good things about it. It's a good way to live with a lot of kids and always have someone to play with. It's also a good way for families to save money and get closer to other people.

Living in a Single-Parent Family

Many kids will live a part of their life in a single-parent family. Most kids find themselves in this situation because their parents have gotten divorced or a parent has died. There are a lot of other things that can cause a kid to be in a single-parent family, including one parent being away on business for a long period of time, one parent being sent to prison or to a hospital, or one parent running away from home and abandoning the family.

Andre lives with his mother in a single-parent family. Because he is an only child, the two of them have gotten to know each other very well. He told us, "I live with my mother and I never met my father. I don't like having just a mother because some things that a father does my mother can't do. I like the situation in some ways because I have more time with my mother and I get to be closer to her."

Caleb lives with his mother and, since his father has recently moved to Florida, he sees him several times a year. This is fine with Caleb, because he was used to living with his mother and likes their situation a lot. He used to have some conflicts with his father and he thinks he will have fewer now because they will see each other less frequently. He likes living in a single-parent family, although since he is an only child, it does get lonely at times.

There are good and bad things about living in a single-parent family. The good things include that you often get more attention from the parent that you do live with and you get to know each other very well. We think that a special kind of trust can come out of this situation and that a kid who lives with just one parent can be a lot more mature one. Parent and child are more free to do things spontaneously, since you don't have to check with a lot of people and, in the situations we've seen, there are fewer family arguments.

There are difficulties in living in a single-parent family. You might miss your other parent a lot and feel that you need him or her for some things. You might get tired of the parent you live with and want a bit more variety. Sometimes the arguments are more intense because you trust each other enough to really fight and you don't have anyone else there to argue with. Some kids find that they have more responsibility when they live in a single-parent family and they don't like this.

If you live in a single-parent family, you should be sure that you and your parent have the kind of relationship you want. In particular, if your parent starts treating you like an adult and talking about adult issues with you — like sex or money problems or politics — you should be sure that you want to talk about these things. Sometimes, when a parent is the only adult in the house, they need to talk about adult issues with someone, so they turn to the kid. This is okay with many of us, because we feel we can handle it and we like being treated like an adult. However, we also like still being a kid and it's important to make sure that you can be a child and do fun and silly things some of the time.

Another problem that can come up in a single-parent family is the parent dating. This is one of the most confusing things for a child to deal with. Most kids who experience this situation find that it happens after their parents have separated or divorced, although some other kids confront a parent's dating after the death of a parent or because they have a parent who has never married. Some kids will never have to deal with this situation, but because it could be a very awkward and sensitive subject between a parent and a child, we think it is important to discuss it honestly.

If your mother started dating after your parents were divorced, you might feel a whole range of confusing emotions: jealousy, anger, relief, embarrassment, resentment, disgust, happiness, sadness. This is because you feel bad that it looks like your parents won't get back together again but good that you mother isn't sitting home and crying all the time. It is important to sit down with a parent and work through some of these feelings.

Caleb told us, "When my mother was dating, it felt strange and unnatural — it didn't seem normal that my parents were seeing anybody other than each other." Another boy in our class said, "I have a parent who is dating. My reaction is mixed because I like the boyfriend, but I would like to see my parents seeing each other, instead of other men or women."

Some parents are scared to tell their children about their new friends because they are afraid of the children's reactions. While this primarily depends on the kids' relationship to the parents and the situation surrounding the dating (separation, divorce, death), we think it is important for parents to tell children when dating begins. It would be awful to find out another way and it wouldn't be good to have a parent develop a close relationship with another person and, after they're all set to move in together, finally tell the kid.

One boy in our class told this story: "One night I was going to my father's house for dinner. The night was unusual, because it was the first time I was to see his new apartment and I was curious. We had just gotten inside and I was looking around when a woman came out of the kitchen and said something about supper to my father. He quickly whispered that I was there and that I did not know about her. He then told me who she was and introduced her as 'someone who spent the night.' This seemed perfectly reasonable to me at the time — I was only eight — but when she spent the next night, and then the next, and I discovered some plates that looked unusual, I was curious, and began to piece things together. I later had to find out for myself who she *really* was (my father's girlfriend), because I had no further explanation."

This way of finding out about parents' dating is difficult for kids and can influence their ability to trust parents. It is important for parents to be honest and clear with children about dating and it is also important for children to be honest back.

We've heard of some parents who take their children along on dates with a new friend. We don't recommend this and would prefer to have a baby-sitter or relative take care of us while our parents are dating. It would be very awkward and uncomfortable for the child, the parent, and the new friend. As Nathan said, "I would not like to be taken along on a date by my mom. I would feel out of place and kind of embarrassed."

Having a friend of the parent sleep over in your home can be a big deal for some kids. Usually, you've met the person before but in some cases this might be the first time you've even seen the person. We talked about how it feels to find out that someone's sleeping over in your house that you really don't know or don't like. One girl in our class said, "When you are younger — like five to eight years old — you feel threatened by this, but when you get older, you understand that your parent needs to have friends too." Matt said, "It is my feeling that children of separated or divorced parents don't really care about this, as long as their parents have been separated for two years or more."

Other kids in our group who had experienced this situation told us, "It is very uncomfortable for single parents to have someone spend the night." One boy said, "When my mom had a friend sleep over the first time, I felt very uncomfortable." Some kids are embarrassed about this, especially if their friends find out; other kids don't mind very much. Stephen told us, "I think older kids don't really mind, especially if the person is nice."

One boy in our class told this story: "I know someone whose parents were separated and he was living with his mom. A man came over and he and my friend got acquainted. The man came over about twice a week and my friend began to like him. Then one morning, my friend woke up and the man was asleep on the couch. My friend pretended that he didn't care, but he told me that he wasn't quite sure whether or not he likes it."

Caleb told us, "Although I have some reservations about friends sleeping over, and from experience know it's a pretty traumatic thing the first time, I feel that ultimately it is the parents' decision and they should decide for themselves. They should at least tell their kids about it and should discuss it with them. Though the child is not directly involved, they will have some interesting feelings about the issue."

The good ways for the parent to deal with dates sleeping over are by discussing it and taking their kids' suggestions and feelings into consideration. If they are good suggestions, they should think about them seriously and perhaps put them into action. Bad ways to deal with this are to be blunt and insensitive with the children or to leave them totally in the dark about the issue. Telling the kids, "Bob and I are going to sleep together tonight, so don't disturb us," won't help much either.

Most of us accept the fact that our parents will need a social life of their own if they are single, and we don't want to impose our feelings and tastes on them. For example, we realize that if we don't like their new boyfriend or girlfriend, we could express our feelings, but we shouldn't act them out very much, like complaining and whining and calling them names and not giving phone messages. If the child does like the parent's new friend, it could be a good situation.

One way to get to know your parent's new friend is by doing things with the friend and your parent. This is different from a date, where the couple is the center of attention. Some of the things that might be fun to do are go to the movies, sporting events, restaurants, plays, or museums. You can all talk about the meal or the event and share your opinions and get to know the person in a safer kind of way than just sitting at home and talking about things. It's also sometimes nice if your parent's new friend is very good at a subject that you are having difficulty with in school — such as math. He or she could help you with your homework in a nice way and make friends through that process.

Another bad part of your parent dating is if you get to like the new friend and then your parent realizes that he or she doesn't. If you've gotten attached to someone who then leaves your life, it could seem almost like a divorce and you might feel ripped off about feelings you've had for the person. This is a risk that you have to think about before you get involved with your parent's new friend.

Dating allows kids to see their parents in a new way. While it can bring up all kinds of confusing and painful feelings, it could also be the start of seeing your parent as a new and independent person. If dating makes your parent happier, we think that it'll make life at home a lot happier for the whole family.

Dealing with a Parent Who Lives Far Away

Some kids in our class have a parent who lives far away. Nate's dad lives in Pennsylvania and he only gets to see him a few times a year. Josh's dad works in Baltimore and he usually only gets to see him on weekends, when he flies back to Boston. Jamey's dad lives in New York, and she sees him on vacations and during the summer.

This kind of situation has special problems. It is sometimes difficult to see a parent who lives far away fully as a parent, because you often don't know them as well as your other parent and you are used to the rules and the personality of your other parent. It can be confusing to visit this parent because he or she might have new rules and expectations that are quite different from those of your other parent. Also, particularly for older kids, seeing a parent who is far away often means you don't get to spend time with your local friends on vacations. This can cause you to feel pulled in two different directions and might bring out some angry feelings. It's also hard because you have to make a whole new set of friends when you visit the parent and your parent often will never get to meet your regular friends or see you at school and meet your teacher.

The good part about having a parent live far away is that you get to travel to different places and sometimes take the bus or the train or the plane by yourself. This can make you feel important and people will make a big fuss over you, especially if you are a little kid.

We think that it is important for parents who live far away to be understanding about their kids and try to keep in touch. We think that they should keep themselves informed about the rules that the kids usually follow, their progress in school, and that they should remember birthdays and special occasions. We also think that they should try to make the time they spend with their kids as normal as possible and, while it's fine for them to give presents and be excited and take the kids out for special dinners, it's also important just to have time together to hang out and act normal.

Holidays are tough times when you have a parent who lives far away. It is ideal if the parent can come to your home for the holiday, especially if both your parents still get along or are still married. If not, you should get to have some say over where you want to spend the holiday and, if you don't get to see the parent on a special occasion, you should definitely be in phone contact. This keeps you feeling connected to both of your parents and makes it clear that they both care about you.

Having a Parent Who Is Gay

Some kids have gay parents. *Gay* refers to people who are sexually interested in others of their own sex, rather than of the other sex. If your parent is like this, he or she is probably gay. Other words for this are *homosexual*, or if the person is female, *lesbian*.

In general, we don't think this is such a big deal. From what we can tell, gay parents are just like other parents. They have their problems and they have their good points. They still fight with us about the food we eat and the clothes we wear and they still take us to the movies.

There are some problems with having a gay parent. You might be ashamed or embarrassed because your parent is different than other parents. You might get teased at school if kids know or you might get embarrassed when people tell "fag" or "dyke" jokes because you feel they are making fun of your parent and they don't know it. Some kids might wonder if they will turn out to be gay, and others might not know much about their own sex, say if you are a boy living with lesbian mothers. You also might worry about how your parent will react if you start dating a person of the other sex.

On the other hand, there are some good aspects to having a gay parent, too. You learn a lot about a different type of relationship and you know that all gays aren't alike and don't fit a stereotype. You also learn to understand about prejudice and how it is used to hurt people and why it is wrong. This can make you a lot more understanding about a lot of people.

Tanya, Becca, and Gillian interviewed Jamey, a girl in our class whose mother is a lesbian. We asked Jamey a lot of questions in order to see if our fears about having a gay parent were reasonable. We learned a lot from her experience:

TBG: (Tanya, Becca, Gillian): How old were you when your mom first told you she was lesbian?

JAMEY: I think she first told me when I was seven.

TBG: What kind of effect did it have on you when you found out?

JAMEY: I was only seven, so I didn't really have a chance to be prejudiced. I hadn't really learned what being gay was, so she had to explain to me what it was and that she *was* gay. It wasn't that big a shock. I really didn't care at the moment. She told me that when I got a little older, I would probably be a little more shocked.

TBG: Does your mother have a girlfriend?

JAMEY: No, not at the moment. I've met two of her girlfriends over the years. It's not like she brings them home to meet me. She might have had other girlfriends, but I don't know.

TBG: Do you feel kind of funny knowing your mom is a lesbian?

JAMEY: Sometimes it can be a little weird. When people crack gay jokes, I'm a little offended because of my mom. It's weird, though, 'cause it doesn't affect me that much. I can laugh at a gay joke and it won't really affect me that much. It really isn't that much different than if my mom wasn't gay.

TBG: Do you and your mom ever talk about it at all?

JAMEY: She had a talk with me a couple of years ago. She was saying that, if I ever had a boyfriend, I shouldn't think that I should have to be gay, just because she is. She said that I should choose for myself. But besides that, we don't talk much about it.

TBG: When you were little and you knew what being lesbian was, did you ever feel like something was wrong with you or your mother?

JAMEY: When I was little, I had a few ideas about gay people, like they were a little weird and all of them were a little stereotypical. When I found out my mom was gay, it kind of erased those ideas (I didn't have strong ideas). I've never been really prejudiced, because learning about gay people erased these ideas from my mind.

TBG: When other people say something rude about being gay, do you ever say something to them? Maybe stick up for it? Or do you leave it alone?

JAMEY: Sometimes I say something if it is really rude or really stupid. I say something like, "Have you ever met anybody like that?" or "Do you know that for a fact?" Then they usually mumble something like "You're right, it probably isn't true." Most of the time it really doesn't bother me.

TBG: Did your parents getting separated have anything to do with your mom being gay?

JAMEY: I think it may have had something to do with it, but I don't think that was all of it.

TBG: Did you think that kids at school were going to tease you?

JAMEY: When she first told me, no. I was going to an alternative program a lot like Fayerweather Street School. I knew another girl in the school — in fact, she was my best friend — and her mother was also a lesbian, so it helped a lot.

When I went into public school in fifth grade, I did worry about it a little. (I had also just moved to Cambridge.) I thought the kids would be a little less open-minded about it. I thought they would tease me. But I found out that if someone was my friend and stopped liking me because my mother was homosexual, then they were not really my friend. I know real friends wouldn't care. It has nothing to do with me, and they would know that. It turned out that nobody did tease me.

TBG: Did you ever feel, after you told your friends, that they put an invisible sign on you saying "my mother is lesbian"?

JAMEY: Well, not really. I was afraid something like that was going to happen. But it never happened.

TBG: Were you ever hesitant about telling friends?

JAMEY: Sometimes, but with most of my friends, I knew they wouldn't care. But there were some people I didn't want to tell.

TBG: Because your mom is lesbian, do you ever feel like you know more about it than other people? And, if so, did that help you at all?

JAMEY: I think I'm a little more open-minded about it. I have to be, it's not like I can say that all gays are weird. But I think in the future, I'm going to be more open-minded than other kids.

TBG: You said you met two of your mother's girlfriends. What did you think of them?

JAMEY: One of my mom's girlfriends I met was actually the mother of my good friend, whose mother was, obviously, also lesbian. It was weird because I was already friends with her daughter, so I had met her mother before. It was kind of strange that her and my mom got together. I think it was partially because of me and Robin. We were always playing together and that's how they met. I liked her.

TBG: Where does your father live?

JAMEY: He lives in New York.

TBG: What does he think about it?

JAMEY: It's not a big deal to him.

TBG: Do you ever talk about it with your dad?

JAMEY: Sometimes, but not very much. I don't really talk about it with anybody really.

TBG: Does your mom have any nongay friends?

JAMEY: Some, of course.

TBG: What do they think of her?

JAMEY: Most don't care.

TBG: Thank you for letting us interview you, Jamey.

Having Only Working Parents

The major issue for children who live with working parents is that they can be home a lot alone or be put in day-care situations. Most of our parents are working parents, because they need the money in order to buy the food we eat and the clothes we wear. Most of our parents also seem to enjoy their work. It usually doesn't cause any problems for kids, but some issues can arise.

When you're young, it can feel scary not to have your parent or parents at home. At an older age, you might be more used to it, so you wouldn't mind as much. Going to day care or having a baby-sitter can be fun, especially if you are in day care and get to spend time with other kids your age.

When John was four, his father would drop him off at day care most days. He liked it a lot because there were other kids to play with and they had a lot of parties. He didn't miss his parents and thought it was "a fun time."

One of the reasons people don't like day care is they think that kids need to spend all their time with their parents. We think that day care teaches kids and parents independence and that you can still spend enough time with your parents.

If you often find yourself alone in the house because your parents are working — especially when you come home from school — we suggest you make a list of the things you enjoy doing and find the time to do them. You could play records loudly or talk on the phone or play games with a friend or sibling. You could also do fun things with a baby-sitter and you could watch television.

Kecia's mom works, and Kecia has a baby-sitter. She gets embarrassed when kids ask her who her baby-sitter is. She finally decided that she would introduce her as "my mother's friend" or "my friend's older sister." This made her feel better — a lot better — and she doesn't mind having her baby-sitter around that much.

If you are in the house alone because your parents are out working (or shopping, for that matter), you should be careful not to do anything dangerous. We recommend that you do not light fires or jump off the roof or any other clearly hazardous activity. We also think you should have a list of emergency phone numbers in case you get in trouble or get scared. If you are angry about being left alone so much, talk to your parents about it and tell them your feelings in a calm way.

It is not unusual or silly for kids to feel scared in the house. Once when Nat was seven years old, he was alone because his father had to work late. He thought he saw a face in the window and got scared. He turned on all the lights in the house, the TV, and radio. When Nat's father got home he asked Nat what was wrong and why everything was on. Nat made up a quick lie. He didn't want to tell him about the face because he thought his father would laugh at him.

Kids who take care of themselves because their parents work are called "latch-key children" (because they have to carry a key to let themselves into the house). If you are this kind of child, we suggest that you put the key someplace where you'll always have it, like on a chain around your neck. There's nothing worse than losing your key and being locked out and unable to reach your parents — especially in winter. You might also hide a key somewhere around your house or apartment or ask a neighbor to keep a spare one in case you need it.

Having parents who work can teach kids a lot of good things, like independence and ways to care for themselves. We feel that it is good for parents to work, even if it does mean that we won't see them as much. It gives the children a better sense of independence and lets the parent have a chance to explore outside the house. While it is also nice to have a parent at home all the time (usually the mother) to give you cookies and talk to you after school, this is a situation that fewer kids find themselves in these days.

Living in a Mixed Racial, Ethnic, or Religious Family

Some kids have parents who are of different races, nationalities, or religious beliefs. To most kids, this is not such a big deal, but because of prejudice and other public responses, we sometimes have to deal with other people's opinions about our parents, which can be uncomfortable to discuss.

Jesse lives with his stepmother and his father. Sometimes he goes to visit his stepmother's family. They go to church every Sunday and Jesse is not used to going to church. He feels out of place when he visits them. He deals with this by feeling strange and avoiding it by not talking about it. Jesse's father is Jewish.

One girl in our class has a mother who is white and is married to a black man. The girl's grandmother doesn't really like it and, while this doesn't cause a big problem, it is sometimes uncomfortable for her.

The good part about having parents of different religions, races, or ethnic backgrounds is that you might get to celebrate different holidays and get to know more about different kinds of people. You might get to travel to different communities and enjoy different traditions, like Italian saints' days or St. Patrick's Day or the Chinese New Year, or you might get to like different kinds of food. Having parents with different backgrounds could also help you see that in spite of racial, ethnic, or religious differences most people are the same in many of the important ways.

Some parents fight about their beliefs or customs and this causes tension for kids. The child of a racially mixed marriage might feel embarrassed about it and keep it secret if they can. There is also sometimes a lot of problems from grandparents because of racial or religious differences and, especially with religion, a lot of fighting about how the child will be brought up.

It's good for parents in this situation to talk about it with the child and not pretend that the situation doesn't exist. Most of this doesn't matter much to kids, who, like their parents, might or might not be interested in the different customs or traditions. We think it is a good idea for parents to expose kids to these customs and let kids decide which ones they want to keep and which ones they want to forget. When the child is older, he or she can make a better decision about these matters.

Being an Only Child

Some of us have no brothers or sisters. We are what is referred to as "only children." There are good things and bad things about being in this position.

If you are an only child, you probably get a lot of attention that you don't have to share with another child. You might also get more presents, clothes, and allowance than you would have if you had brothers or sisters. And you don't get into fights with brothers or sisters, since you don't have any.

There are some drawbacks to being an only child. Sometimes you get lonely and wish there was another kid to play with, or you could get into fights with your parents and have no other kids to take your side. If you live with both your parents, you might feel that, in lots of situations, it turns out to be two people against one, with no one supporting you. You don't have older siblings to help you with your homework or to do some of the major chores around the house. Also, you might find that you have more family responsibilities than kids with larger families.

Your relationship with your parents is somewhat different if you're an only child. You probably are closer to them than other kids are and you probably get a chance to do more things with them and not have other people distract their attention from you. Some only children tend to be spoiled by their parents.

One of the things we like most about being an only child is that you can do fun activities with your parents and not have to share them with another child. One girl we know went shopping one day with her mother, they had lunch together and they had no fights. If you had siblings, the odds are that they would come with you and cause problems.

John sometimes doesn't like to be an only child because

Being an only child can make you close to your parent.

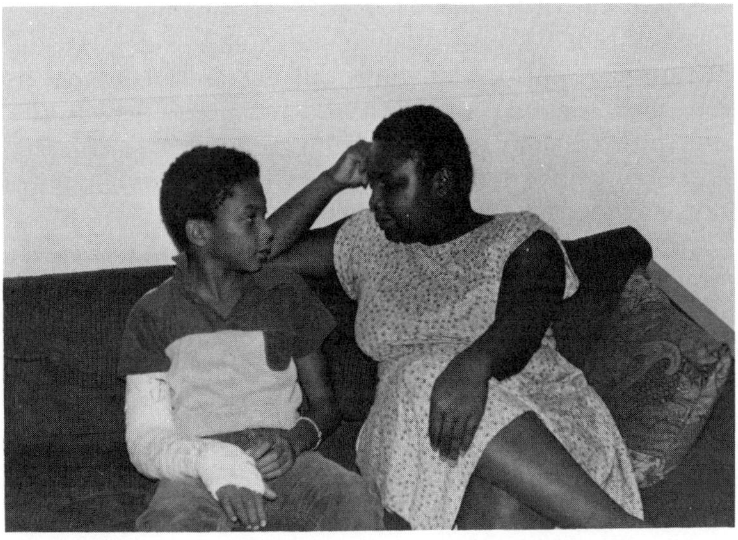

his parents are busy and he often gets bored. If he had a brother or sister, he'd have someone to play with more often. Andre feels the same way. He sometimes plays an Atari game with his mother and he wishes that he had someone else to play with — mainly because she is not very good at the game.

Some of us like being an only child. Caleb likes getting so much attention and the fact that his mother gets to spend so much time with him and helps with the activities he likes. Macy also enjoys being an only child and feels that she is closer to her parents because of it.

Dealing with Siblings

Having a brother or a sister or many brothers and sisters can cause problems that involve parents. Parents sometimes have a favorite child and this makes everyone tense and competitive. Children sometimes fight amongst themselves and the parents end up having to take sides or settle the problem. Also, sometimes all the children have to share their parents' attention and never get time to develop individual relationships with parents. This situation is especially hard if the parent doesn't have a lot of money and the kids all want different clothes and different toys.

There are some good things about having siblings. Sometimes it's fun to do something nice for a brother or a sister and you can collaborate with your parent and make this a very special treat for the sibling. You can also do some things that are fun and that couldn't be done without more people — like board games or sports.

In general, we think that the major problem that comes up is when there is fighting between two kids and the parent tries to get involved and solve things. This can create problems for everyone. If you are in this situation, we think you should tell your parent that, if it looks like an argument might accomplish something and the kids can finish it themselves, the parent should butt out. Only if it looks very destructive or as if it might become violent should the parent become involved. This teaches kids to take responsibility for themselves and solve problems as they arise.

If you think that your parent is playing favorites with one of your brothers or sisters, we think you should think about it carefully. It might seem this way to you, just because you don't always get everything you want, but often it is not the case. If you have a lot of clear evidence that they have a favorite child, you should speak to them honestly about it and see if you could correct the situation.

One problem that often comes up in a family is the birth of a baby. This can make kids very happy and very excited but it can also cause jealousy and cause the older brother or sister to feel that too much work, chores, and babysitting is expected. If you have a new brother or sister and you feel like your parent is not paying enough attention to you, please try to be understanding and realize that new babies need a lot of attention. If the situation is bad enough to make you very unhappy, talk to your parent. Parents really do need to find a way to continue to have time with the older child, even when a new baby is born.

There are some funny things that happen when you have brothers and sisters. Kate told us that her grandmother's birthday celebration had been postponed until there was a time when the whole family could come together for it. Her little sister Holly woke up in the middle of the night, went to the kitchen, and sliced up the birthday cake and served it, with butter, to herself and her dolls. This was a funny but unhappy situation for everyone involved (since they needed the cake for the real party).

Parents can resolve some of the problems that come up between siblings with creative solutions. When Jonathan had just started baby-sitting for his sister, she would scream and shout when their parents would leave because she thought that he'd be mean to her once they were alone. Then his parents decided that they'd pay her $1 if she behaved while they were gone. This got her to behave herself (and Jonathan too), and now Jonathan and his sister sometimes even have fun together.

PART V

Dealing with Serious Problems

In Part 2, we discussed the problems that face most kids and parents, the issues we think most children need to resolve with their parents. Although all kids we know don't have problems with their parents on issues such as bedtime, sleepovers, or television rules, most have some kind of conflicts in these areas.

Some children, however, face particular situations that most of us never have to deal with. Often these situations can involve real crises — such as being beaten up by a parent or having to deal with a parent who is drunk all the time. In this section, we look at the special problems that some children have and we try to offer helpful suggestions and good advice.

Keep in mind that, even if your own family doesn't have one of the problems mentioned in here, it is important for you as a child to be aware of them. You might have a friend who has one of these problems. Some day, for one reason or another, you will probably wish you'd thought about these things. We hope all children will read this section and try to understand what it is like for kids who have to deal with these serious issues all the time.

Having a Parent Who Abuses Drugs or Alcohol

Our class watched a movie called *Francesca, Baby*. In the movie, Francesca, the oldest child in a family that has just moved to a California suburb, has a mother who became an alcoholic when her youngest child, Robbie, died. Francesca's father travels a lot and is rarely home for long periods of time or special occasions and holidays. Francesca is in a difficult position in her family. She is forced to act as a mother to her younger sister, Katie, and is also taking care of her mother, who is usually too drunk to do the things that most parents do. In addition to all of this pressure, Francesca has to put up with the embarrassment of her mother being drunk and doing humiliating things in front of her friends.

Finally, after trying to confront her mother and get her to stop drinking, Francesca goes to a group called Alateen, where many kids her age share their feelings and discuss the problems related to having alcoholic relatives. This makes Francesca realize that she can't solve her mother's problem and that she needs to find a way to continue living with an alcoholic parent and yet not let her life be ruined.

At first, Francesca's mother is very angry that her daughter is attending this group, but then she realizes that her daughter has found a way to help herself and perhaps she, the mother, could also help herself. Francesca's mother calls Alcoholics Anonymous to arrange for some kind of help, and the movie ends with a bit of optimism and hope.

Most of us liked this movie and found it very helpful in

understanding some of the problems related to having an alcoholic parent. Some of us know kids in this situation and some of us have only read about it in newspapers or seen situations like Francesca's on TV shows and news reports. We have also had different experiences with having parents abuse drugs or alcohol and have a wide range of reactions to these situations.

We've looked at a couple of dictionary definitions of "alcoholism," all of which seemed pretty complicated and scientific to us. Macy thinks that "being an alcoholic means that you can't handle the intake of alcohol, and because of this, it starts to affect other family members and friends." Kate thinks, "Alcoholics are people who have too many alcoholic beverages on a regular basis. For instance, they might begin to drink in the morning and by the time they go to sleep are more often than not drunk. If a person did this every day or almost every day, I would consider him or her an alcoholic." Jamey thinks that an alcoholic is someone who "needs a drink to feel comfortable." It is clear to us that alcoholics lose control over themselves and that the alcohol itself tends to take over.

We talked about what advice we should give to children who have parents who abuse alcohol or drugs. It's important to realize that it is *not* your fault and that it is the parent's problem and he or she will have to realize this and get help. As Gillian put it, "You can try helping your parents, but do get help yourself." After you've taken care of yourself, by getting into a group like Alateen or talking to your counselor, you might want to encourage your parent to get professional help or to join Alcoholics Anonymous.

Many of us have seen our parents drinking and some have seen our parents smoking marijuana. Most of us feel comfortable with this unless they get really drunk and out of control or start using hard drugs. Mike told us, "If I saw one of my parents drunk — really drunk — I don't think I could handle it. It would be depressing for me to see my parents using hard drugs." Jamey said, "I think it would be scary to see a parent drunk or on drugs, because you usually consider your parent to be in control." Gillian told us, "If a parent used drugs a lot, I would get sort of mad, but if they were doing drugs just a little, I really wouldn't care."

Justin thinks that some children might feel influenced to take drugs if they see their parents shooting up or doing all kinds of pills. He also said, "The child might feel like it's something to hide," and be ashamed of his parents. Joy said, "If I saw any parent drunk, I would feel scared, disappointed, nervous, and sad. If I saw a parent taking drugs, I would be really upset at them."

We know that teenagers a little older than us often feel differently about drugs and alcohol than we do. We think this might be because they are less connected to their parents than we are. But drugs and alcohol tend to be a scary subject for younger children.

One boy in our class told us, "My family had to take care of my cousin because her mother was having drinking problems and was unable to take care of her. I felt sorry for her, but in a couple of weeks, the problem had been taken care of and now she seems to be fine." Alcoholism is a real problem when parents lose the ability to be parents and the kids have to go to other relatives or, even worse, become the parents themselves. Joy heard about a story involving a mother of two kids who drank at lot. One night this woman was acting very strange and behaving dangerously. She flipped her lid and almost killed the youngest child.

It can be confusing for kids to be told not to use drugs or not to drink alcohol by a parent who abuses alcohol or drugs. Kate thinks that these kinds of parents will set a bad example for kids of any age, but especially older kids, since they may also be subjected to the pressure of their peers. Ana said, "People who live in glass houses shouldn't throw stones." Some of us would think our parents hypocrites if they told us not to do something that they did themselves. We know that some people feel it's worse for kids to use drugs than adults because adults are supposedly "more in control" of themselves, but some of us think that alcohol and drug abuse is dangerous, regardless of age.

If you are at a friend's house and it is obvious that his or her parent is drunk or doing drugs, you should be careful about how you react because this is already a tough situation for your friend and you can either make it worse or make it better. John says, "Do not freak out or anything like that. Humor your friend's parent unless your friend tells you otherwise." Kate said, "Friends can be most helpful by remaining calm and trying to help with the parent in any way they can. Afterward, you might say something like, 'My parents have gotten drunk too,' but you shouldn't lie about it. If you can't say something like that, you might say something like, 'Don't worry about it, these things happen.' " Comfort your friend and be there if he or she needs someone to talk to.

If your parent abuses drugs or alcohol, there are some kinds of behavior that you should consider unacceptable:

A parent should never accuse a child of being the reason why they drink or do drugs.

In most cases, parents should never get drunk or stoned in the presence of a child's friends.

Parents should never offer their children drugs or alcohol — especially when they are already drunk or high.
A child should never be put in the position where he or she has to get a cab and push the parent into it to get home.
A parent should never drive a car when high or drunk.

If your parents do any of these things, we recommend that you speak to them about it immediately and find a solution to the problem. This is when abuse of drugs or alcohol can become a kind of psychological child abuse.

Facing Child Abuse and Neglect

One of the most difficult things for a child to deal with is child abuse. If you are abused by a parent — whether physically, verbally, emotionally, or sexually — you might feel so ashamed about it that you'd never tell anyone it is happening to you. You also might think that this is your parents' legal right, that because they are your parents they can do things like beat you, burn you, or rape you. This is not true. There are actually laws that protect children from this kind of abuse. The hard part for kids is to find a way to get out of this awful situation because most kids feel so conflicted and embarrassed about what is going on that they don't do anything about it.

Child abuse and neglect are generally two different things. We think it is important for kids to know what kinds of things are considered to be abuse and what kinds of things are simply reasonable (though we might hate them) kinds of punishments. Abuse tends to be violent — kids are badly hurt by a parent or other relative — and this violence can be physical (whippings, biting, burning, punching), verbal (regular excessive yelling, threats, humiliation, viciously telling a child that they "were a mistake''), sexual (getting raped, forced to touch an adult somewhere you don't want to touch them, being kissed or touched in ways you don't want to), and emotional. To neglect a child is to let the child go without adequate clothing or not give them proper food or feed them regularly. It could involve leaving young children for long periods of time or not taking care of a child's medical problems.

We made a list of some of the things that we would consider to be child abuse or child neglect. We did this so kids could know what kinds of behavior they should not accept from their parents and because we wanted kids to know that even if their parents say ''all kids get tortured by their parents'' this is not so. We find these things unacceptable:

hitting a child powerfully, especially in the head, face, or genitals
kicking a child
throwing a child down the stairs
trying to rape a child
forcing a child to take drugs
tying a child up or locking them in a room
burning a child
constantly yelling unfairly and unexpectedly at a child
scratching a child
not getting a child appropriate clothing (like winter coats) so the child gets sick or humiliated
not providing food for the child at mealtimes

There are other activities that most of us think are wrong, but we would not put them in the category of child abuse or child neglect, because, although they are harmful to the child, they are not as dangerous (except when done in excess) as most abuse. For example, raping a child once will probably have long-term effects on the child but grounding a child for one week probably won't. Here is a list of things that we don't consider to be abuse or neglect, although some people might:

occasional spankings
spoiling a child
slapping a child
sending a child up to his or her bedroom during dinner
wrestling with the child
yelling at a child who does something wrong
making a child do a lot of chores
grounding the child

Abuse and neglect confuse kids because they wonder how a person who loves them can also hurt them and do bad things to them. We feel like a mixed message, which is very difficult for kids to deal with, is sent with child abuse. Child abuse seems to come from parents who are angry or disturbed or who were abused or neglected themselves when they were young. Parents who are under stress and out of control might take it out on those they have the most power over — their children. It's a lot easier for parents to yell or hit children than it is for them to yell at their boss. Most parents who abuse their children feel that they are out of control and it is not their fault, but it's important for kids to realize that it *is* their parent's fault and they have a responsibility to control themselves and find another way of dealing with their angry feelings.

What should you do if you find yourself in a situation where you are experiencing abuse? For example, what can you do if you did something wrong and your parent comes at you with a big stick and you think he or she is going to batter you badly? Well, we don't have all the answers, but we have some clear suggestions. First, it's important to try to save yourself from the physical pain of the abuse. Get as far away from the parent as possible until he or she cools off. You might go to a neighbor's house or just run out of your apartment or house and walk around the streets. Just get out of there. One kid we knew would hide in a closet and his parents wouldn't be able to find him. Joachim suggests, "If a kid is about to be beaten by an adult, *stare* at the adult and ask him or her why they're doing it. If you don't have the guts to do this, then just run."

If you are in a situation where you are often afraid of being abused, you should talk to someone. David said, "If the kid is old enough he or she should call a friend or call a place that helps people with problems like that. I would be careful that the parent doesn't find out." This is the difficult part because many kids are afraid that if they call a relative or neighbor or the police the parent will find out and react with even more violence. Still, we think it's important to find another adult to talk to, someone who can connect you with the services and clinics that deal with child abuse. If you live in a big city, there are probably a lot of service centers near you. If you don't, you should look in the phone book under things like "Child Abuse Hotline" or "Parental Stress Line" or "Parents Anonymous," which is a group that helps parents who feel like getting violent with their kids.

Matt said, "If you find that your parent is abusing you, you should let a neighbor know, or your teacher. You could also go to a clinic." Kate suggests, "Perhaps the school nurse, who can look at the marks and treat them medically, can suggest what you can do about this."

Even though it is scary to get another adult involved in this situation, we feel that ultimately it will benefit the child and the parent. Caleb told us, "If this is one of the many abusive things the parent does, the child should definitely get outside help, preferably from a place that specifically deals with abuse, rather than the police. If this is the first time, the kid probably should talk to the parent when they are finally calm enough to listen. The most important part is that the parent know what he or she is doing and that it is wrong. If possible, the child should search for a shelter that deals especially with children who are being abused. Good friends, people you know, or family doctors are also some good, easily accessible people who will be able to help. Going to the police is probably not the best idea. They might do more hurt than help and could very well confuse or even frighten an abused child."

We've seen other kids in abusive situations and sometimes felt like we have been unable to go to the adult and tell them what they were doing was wrong. Unfortunately, they'd probably start abusing us and it's probably more helpful if another adult confronts them with the situation. Joachim told us, "When a group of kids and I went to see the movie *The Outsiders*, there was a woman with a child who fell down on the sidewalk. The mother screamed at her child to get up off the dirty sidewalk and was also screaming obscenities at the child. I really wanted to tell the woman to stop."

One girl in our class used to baby-sit for a woman who locks her son into his bedroom when he won't take a nap. The boy screams and cries and kicks the door. Whenever this girl put him to bed, he would cry "Don't lock that door!" We could tell that this was having a damaging effect on him.

If you are in a situation where your parent is neglecting you, try to find out why. If they have to work all the time and have no time to take care of you, perhaps another relative or friend could help out.

Neglect is a lot less obvious to kids than abuse, but it is important to notice it when it occurs and find a way to put a stop to it. Sometimes it helps to tell a parent that you need them to care about the clothing you wear or you need them to feed you better.

Responding to Incest and Sexual Abuse

It is very difficult to talk about incest and sexual abuse because it can be embarrassing and uncomfortable and many kids who experience this kind of abuse block it out and pretend it doesn't happen. Unfortunately, many children — of all ages — are taken advantage of by adults. We're including this section in our book, because we think it's important for kids to recognize that adults do not have the right to touch us in a sexual way against our will.

Ana was in court one day on a separate matter, and she saw a case prosecuted that involved a man who raped his three-year-old stepdaughter. Some of us have heard about a book and television show called *Peyton Place,* which involved a girl who had slept with her father and became pregnant. We have also read stories and seen news reports about strangers who molest kids, older brothers who abuse younger siblings, and gang rapes of young women. These stories scare us and make us very uncomfortable.

We think it is important to know that no one has the right to touch you in a sexual way, or make you touch them, or have sexual intercourse with you, or just act sexy with you, when you don't want them to.

We talked about what rape actually is. Matthew said that rape is an act of violence. Ana said, "What I feel is rape is when a person forces someone else to have any kind of sexual activity that you don't want to have, or if a child is under eighteen and having sex with an adult."

Caleb thinks it's important for kids to watch out for strangers because they tend to be the most unpredictable people you will come across. Parents — especially fathers, stepfathers, boyfriends, uncles, even grandfathers — can also take advantage of kids sexually. Of course, most parents don't and, for most kids, incest (which involves sexual relations between family members) isn't an issue. But if you are in a situation where someone is doing things to you that you don't like, it's important to find the courage to do something about it.

Miguel thinks that you should go right to the police and report what happened. Jesse thinks that this would be hard to do, especially if you were reporting on your father and you loved him a lot. Matthew suggests calling a child abuse hotline or special child abuse agency, and Ana thought that it is best to visit a clinic that specializes in sexual abuse. In any case, it's important to realize that if someone takes advantage of you sexually — whether they threaten to kill you or do it by giving you candy and nice things — it is not your fault and you do not have to put up with it.

If you are assaulted by a stranger, you should go to your parents. Don't let them blame you and tell you it's your fault. Get medical help and understanding. They shouldn't force you to go to the police if you don't want to, but we think you really should consider talking with the police because the same person could just go on molesting other kids. It's also important that you don't ignore what has happened or pretend that it never happened, even though you think it might be easier just to wipe it out of your mind. The danger in this is that it could happen again, either to you or to someone else.

If you are concerned about a sexually abusive incident, either with an adult that you know or a stranger, find someone to talk to — a teacher, friend of the family, or a neighbor. Talking may not be the answer to your problem but it might help you feel better until you find a real answer. You don't have to feel ashamed or that it's your fault that this happened, and you don't have to feel that it's your job to save the adult's reputation. Your basic job is to make sure that this kind of thing doesn't happen again and that adults learn to understand that taking advantage of kids and forcing them to do things they really don't want to do is wrong.

Preventing Parent Abuse

Many of our parents complain that we abuse them. Most of us don't. We act moody at times and don't do our chores, but this isn't what we mean when we talk about parent abuse. Some kids — especially teenagers — abuse their parents in dangerous, even physical, ways. Parents of children like this are so embarrassed that they don't tell anyone, and instead are frightened of their kids and the kids get away with murder.

Joachim told us this story: "When I was in Virginia, I went to camp. There was one kid there — he didn't go to the camp, but his brother did — and whenever his mother would get her paycheck, he would take the money. He was constantly abusing her and broke her leg. No one stopped him. This guy was around seventeen."

Jesse told us another story. He knows a boy who was always getting into violent fights with his family. One time he broke his mother's arm and his sister's arm. The family had him arrested and he was sent to a military academy to be reformed.

Parent abuse is a weird thing, almost hard to imagine. Ana said, "When I first heard about parent abuse, I couldn't believe it. Kids can't abuse their parents, simply because they're the parents. But then I heard about some grandchildren who locked their grandparents in closets and wouldn't let them out for days. It's not very publicized, but you realize that some teenagers are a lot bigger and stronger than their parents."

If you are a kid who abuses parents, we urge you not to do it. Get some kind of help and find a better way to express your anger. All of us feel really angry and even want to get violent toward our parents at some time. But all of us find something else to do with these feelings that doesn't amount to parent abuse. Caleb suggests that kids like this "take care of the anger in another way. You can be very angry at a parent and not participate in abuse. Get a punching bag, if you have to hit something."

PART VI

Becoming a Teenager

Thinking About Being an Adult

Around the time that you begin to become a teenager, you may notice that your parents begin to act strangely toward you. They may begin to make quick, off-the-cuff remarks to you, such as "My little baby is growing up!" or "Soon you'll leave us and never see us again." If you notice this happening, you should realize that your parents are beginning to feel sad about the fact that you are growing up and will most likely be leaving home one day.

Our parents seem to have all kinds of confused feelings about our growing up and leaving home. Jesse said, "Parents seem to worry about their kids growing up and leaving home because they're afraid their kids won't be able to make it on their own." Kristin noticed, "My mom acts like she's lost her little baby. She gets all quiet and doesn't want to be bothered and makes herself look very sad."

Macy told us about something different. She said, "I think parents feel two things when their child leaves home. One thing is that they feel happy because they can have more time to themselves, but I think they feel sad also to see their little child grown up and gone." Caleb noticed, "All parents seem to believe, deep inside, that their life will fall apart when all their children have left home. The best way they seem to react though — at least in front of their kids — is that growing up is a part of adulthood, and that, even though leaving home will hurt them, it is an important step in life."

If parents have mixed feelings about kids becoming adults, we also have these feelings. Some of us worry about how we will be able to survive on our own. Becca used to get scared and wonder where she would get a job and how she would make money. As she got older, though, she became much less worried. Nathan starts freaking out when he thinks about dealing with income taxes and, whenever Josh has too much homework or feels overworked at school, he starts wishing that he were a kid again and was being taken on rides on the Swan Boats in the Boston Public Garden.

Caleb starts feeling a little overwhelmed when he thinks about being an adult. He told us, "I realize I'm going to have to do all these things, like go shopping, buy food, and get a job. It's hard for me to believe that when I grow up I will have the kind of responsibilities that every adult deals with every day. I frequently have questions like, 'How will I learn about taxes and balancing my checkbook?' Does it just happen magically when I become eighteen?"

Some of us realize that, even though we're only eleven, twelve, or thirteen, we're no longer the innocent little kids we once were. Macy thinks about this when she is babysitting for younger children. She wishes that she was a little kid again, going to the playground and having a good time. Others of us sometimes feel a little jealous of the younger kids in our school and the fact that they don't really worry about some of the things that we have to worry about.

Another feeling that many of us have about growing up involves guilt. We feel a little guilty sometimes that we're becoming more independent of our parents and that we don't need them in the same way we did when we were little kids. Nathan told us, "I feel that when I grow up, I won't have enough time to spend with my mom. This makes me feel very guilty. I still don't know how to handle these feelings." Kristin has similar feelings. She told us, "Sometimes I feel guilty because my parents will probably miss me a lot. I guess this is either because I'm the youngest kid in my family, or I'm so wonderful. Anyway, I make plans in my mind to live next door to them or down the street."

If you have these guilty feelings, you should talk about them with your parents, but you should realize that the feelings will probably be around for a while. As Caleb put it, "Guilty feelings never go away, but they decrease as both the kid and the parent realize that growing up and leaving home is a natural part of life."

Some of us feel only very good feelings about getting older and becoming adults. Ana, for example, feels excited about growing up and can't wait to start her new life as an adult. Jesse told us, "I feel good thinking about growing up and leaving home because, right now, I want my own space." Josh feels well prepared for life as an adult and told us, "My parents have taught me about everything that parents should teach, such as sex and also a nonbiased drug education course. They've also given me books about growing up that have helped me."

There are many things that parents should do to help prepare kids for growing up and the responsibilities of being an adult. They should certainly talk to us about responsibility, sex, and marriage. They should teach us how to cook, do laundry, and deal with money and taxes and bills. They should also be sure to give us the freedom to try things on our own, make mistakes, and learn from these mistakes.

Josh told us, "Parents should let their kids grow and develop naturally and not restrict them. They should talk with the kids as much as possible. It is also important that they not ignore the fact that sex, drugs, violence, and other things are happening around the kids, and that kids need to know about these things."

Macy had some specific suggestions for what parents should do. She told us, "One good thing for parents to do is to let you come to work with them for a day, just to see what you might be doing some day. Another thing a parent could do is to make the child pay for something that a parent ordinarily pays for. Parents can also choose to do nothing to help children grow up, letting the kids fend for themselves. This has risks, however."

If you have an older brother or sister who has left home already, it might be a little easier for you because your parents have probably dealt with the situation and have already worked through some of their feelings about their kids growing up and leaving. Nathan told us, "I think it is easier for me, being the youngest child in my family, because I already have my brother as an example of how to grow up."

If you live in a single-parent family — especially if you are an only child — you might feel awful about leaving your parent all alone. If you have a big family, or if your parents are together, it might be a little easier on you. If you have a parent who says things to you like "Oh, Timmy, someday you'll get sick of me and want to move out and live on your own!" you'd find it especially hard to grow up and leave them.

We think that the issues facing children as they enter adolescence need to be discussed with parents. This is hard, because adolescence is sometimes a very rocky time between parents and kids. Parents and kids should discuss their feelings about growing up and reaching puberty. It is good for parents to be honest about their feelings from the start, but to avoid laying heavy guilt trips. It's also important for them to say how much they are going to miss us — and not as a joke or in a humorous manner. No matter what, parents shouldn't try to keep children younger than they are or try to overly control them during their teenage years.

In this section of the book, we discuss some of the key issues that come up with teenagers and their parents. Since most of us are eleven, twelve, and thirteen, we are on the younger end of the teenage years and our perspective is limited. Some of us have older brothers and sisters and older friends, so we've seen the problems that older teens have with their parents.

We don't think that the teenage years have to be an awful time between parents and their kids, but we do think that parent-child relationships change a lot at this time. We believe that all children need to grow up during adolescence and try to be honest and open with their parents, realizing that they will no longer see their parents as the superheroes or perfect people they used to be. There is still a need for parents to support their kids and give them advice and sometimes set limits, but we do think that most of the relationship should be focused on helping kids take responsibility for themselves.

Parents can help by allowing kids to have more input into family decisions and decisions about their own lives. It is also helpful for parents to talk about their own experiences as adolescents, as long as they don't expect their child to be the exact same teenager that they were. Parents need to keep in mind that times change and issues change and the most important thing they can do is to teach their kids to deal with the issues that come up in their lives in a responsible and healthy way.

Dealing with Change

One of the things that could help kids and parents with many of the problems that come up in the teenage years is the ability to deal with change. Most of us had never really thought about how we deal with change in our lives and in our families' lives before we worked on this book, but it seems to us now that this is an important skill for people to have if they are going to survive the problems in teenage years.

Throughout a child's life, families have to deal with big changes, some of which can be very shocking and difficult — such as divorce, death, a parent losing a job, a parent coming out as gay. For many people, change itself is difficult and even minor changes that seem unimportant to many of us — such as getting a new car, changing the time you eat dinner, or wearing new clothing — are quite difficult and bring about fights in the family.

Kate told us, "I personally find it hard to deal with change. The reason is because, when I moved up to the Boston area from New Jersey, I cried the whole summer and most of September. Whenever my mother said, 'Let's go home,' I said, 'You mean home — New Jersey?!' I cried at not being in New Jersey and also not being with my grandmother."

On the other hand, Tanya thinks she deals with change well. She said, "I am a person who deals with change well because I always try to look on the bright side."

We think that it is important for kids and parents to look

at how they deal with changes before some of the major changes of adolescence start happening. Some changes that occur in adolescence involve shifts in the parent/child relationship; physical and sexual changes; changes in friendships; and new attitudes toward drugs, alcohol, careers, cars, and the telephone.

There are some things that people can do to help them deal with changes comfortably. Justin told us, "I would advise kids just to hang on and bear with the changes. They might take a lot of getting used to, but you will adjust to things in time."

Tanya thinks that kids should look at changes as optimistically as possible and see in them the opportunity for positive things to happen. Joachim feels this way as well and said, "Kids should accept the change as a change for the better."

Elizabeth thinks that there are three ways to deal with change. "One way is to be pessimistic about everything and whine and yell and sulk. This may be the way you feel if it is a 'bad' change, and you don't like it, but it does nothing to make you feel better. The second way is to be optimistic and say to yourself, 'Everything will be just fine and great' — but that's not realistic. Finally, you could look at the problem from both angles and play it by ear — hour by hour and day by day. Whenever it's practical to do this, it seems to work."

Some of us have had helpful experiences with difficult changes in our lives. Kate told us, "When I moved up here from New Jersey and I was miserable, my mother sent me to New Jersey to visit every weekend and every vacation. To me, that was very helpful, because then I could be sure to be with my grandmother, even though I had moved far away."

Jonathan remembers that, when his granddad died, the

whole family was very supportive of each other, which helped with the changes in the family.

One thing that seems to help kids with changes is if the change is not made to seem even more important than it really is. Sometimes kids (and parents) exaggerate a change and make it very dramatic and awful. Some changes deserve this kind of treatment, but most don't. So it helps if everyone could be realistic about how big a change it is. The same is true for pretending a big change is not so big. This helps fool no one.

It also helps if kids don't feel sorry for themselves and mope and whine a lot. This can drive other kids and adults crazy and makes the problem even worse. This doesn't mean that you shouldn't see a problem as a problem and wish that it didn't have to happen to a good person like yourself. You shouldn't do this for very long, however, and you certainly shouldn't keep complaining about a change that you can't prevent.

The biggest reason that people need to find a way to deal with changes is that many of them can't be prevented and some of them shouldn't be prevented. Changes can make your life exciting and show you are a growing person. Being afraid of change could result in your leading a life of nervousness and paranoia. Dealing with change well could help you make each change work for your own benefit.

Telephone Use

One of the first changes that many people notice when kids start to become teenagers is the way they use the telephone. Most kids we know don't talk on the phone very much or for very long until they are ten or eleven years old. Some teenagers we know don't talk on the telephone very much either, but many of us spend more time on the phone now than we did when we were a few years younger.

Why do some teenagers talk on the phone so much? Macy thinks it is because they want to know what's going on with their classmates and friends after school hours. Gillian thinks that it is because they find it more enjoyable to talk on the phone than face-to-face, and Heidi thinks it is because they have a lot to talk about. Nat doesn't know why and said to us, "Your guess is as good as mine."

It seems obvious to us that when kids begin to get more sociable with their friends, the telephone becomes more appealing because though you can't easily get to see some of your friends after school it is easy to reach them by picking up the telephone. The telephone is a safe and fun way to communicate, especially before kids know how to drive or are comfortable traveling on public transportation.

We think there are some things parents can do to make living with a teenager who likes to talk on the phone a lot more manageable. Here are our suggestions:

Tell them not to gab for hours.
Insist that friends not call when everyone is asleep.
Limit long-distance calls or insist the teenager pay for them.
Set a time limit, especially when others need the phone.
Don't let phone use interfere with homework.
Don't allow anyone to make phony phone calls.

We think some telephone rules we've heard of are very unfair. For example, limiting calls to one minute seems unreasonable for anyone — especially teens. We also think it's unreasonable to take all phone privileges away from kids: There are some times when phone use is really necessary (like getting some homework help). We also think that installing a pay phone in the house — which

Talking on the phone for hours can annoy the rest of your family.

some of our parents have threatened to do — isn't a good idea.

Kecia told us this story: "I was at a friend's house and her boyfriend called to find out if she would like to go to the movies. Her telephone time was up. She told him she couldn't go to the movies and was suggesting an alternate plan when her father came and just hung the phone up." We think this is unfair and that it shows a parent abusing power. There are better ways to handle the situation than hanging up on someone. Handing the kid little notes that say "Get off the phone *now*!" is much more reasonable, as is simply nagging them till they get off.

Some families attempt to solve some of these telephone problems by buying a phone for the kid. Most families can't afford this expense and sometimes it doesn't solve the problem because kids end up on the phone all the time and the parent still has to set limits and fights still occur. But some of us do have our own phones and deal with the situation reasonably and conflicts about phones have lessened in our families.

We believe that parents should never listen in on phone conversations by picking up an extension and eavesdropping. Even if it is not an important conversation full of big secrets, this kind of behavior can seriously damage a child's ability to trust a parent. It is as dangerous as reading a kid's mail or looking in a diary. Parents should resist this temptation. If they are curious about the conversation, they should ask their child afterward. Eavesdropping is just no good.

Since talking on the phone is a nice way to be with friends when you can't *really* be with them, we think that it is a good way for teenagers to socialize. Finding ways to do this and not drive your parent crazy takes some real skills but will really make teenage life a lot easier.

Changing Friendships

As children become teenagers, their friendships change in several ways. When we were children, a friend was mainly someone to do something with when our parents were busy. We didn't really care that much about our friends' opinions and we didn't spend very much time with our friends.

As we get older, our friendships become more important to us. We care a lot about what our friends think about things — such as clothing, sports, and our other friends. They have a greater influence on us than they did before, and we tend to spend a lot more time with them — after school, on weekends, and on vacations.

Our relationships with our parents change also. Most teenagers we know spend a lot of time with their friends and only a little time with parents. A lot of this change has to do with kids needing to establish our own independent identities and no longer be "Patty's daughter" or "José's little girl." Tanya told us that she spends more time with her friends and less time with her parents now that she is thirteen. She said, "My friends and I share more interests now. Also, I now realize that my parents aren't always right about everything."

Kids should feel fine about spending more time with their friends, especially as they get to be old enough to travel around town on their own and aren't dependent on their parents. We do recommend, however, that you find a way to still spend some time with your parents. Teenagers are old enough to take a more active role in planning family outings and other events, and can even mention new things to do to parents. So, it's a good idea to make sure that you spend some quality time with your parents — not just time spent fighting about clothing or cars.

There are some nasty sides to adolescent friendships for which kids need to be prepared. Parents can help you with this. Adolescents can tease each other a lot and some of it is very painful. Kids also talk behind each other's backs and make fun of people in bad ways. We don't recommend that parents butt into our lives and have a say in all these things, but we do think parents can help out in extreme situations by talking to you about the problems and giving a fresh perspective on the situation.

Peer pressure may also be a difficult issue. This involves

strong influence from your friends that can take the form of jokes, criticisms, and nagging. Kecia told us about how peer pressure has influenced her: "When I started the school year in this class, I really didn't pay much attention to how I dressed, but now I care more about how I look." She thinks that the influence of her friends and other kids in the class pressured her into caring more about her appearance. Peer pressure can also influence kids on issues such as drugs and alcohol, sex, cheating in school, shoplifting, and name-calling.

Most of us care a lot about what our peers think and, therefore, peer pressure may be very influential for us. However, we do think that as a teenager you need to make decisions on your own and not let classmates and friends force you into doing things you don't want to do. Even if they are going to call you names because you don't smoke — or something like that — you'll feel more honest toward yourself if you don't give in. If you do give in and you regret it later, that's okay. It should help you be stronger the next time around.

Issues such as dating, going steady, sexuality, and love also come up when you become a teenager. We can't tell you a whole lot about these things, since most of us are too young to have been involved in them. But we don't think that kids should rush into these things. You should decide when you are ready to start dating and have boyfriends and girlfriends and not worry if everyone's doing it and you don't feel like it.

While most of us cared a lot about what our parents thought of our friends when we were children, we are more independent now and care less about our parents' opinions of our friends. We want our parents to be less involved in our friendships and trust us to make decisions and to make mistakes and learn from them. Kecia gave us an example of this: "When I was nine years old, if I wanted to go to the movies with a friend, I'd ask my mom to take us. Now I just ask my mom if we can go. I don't want her to be as actively involved in my friendships as I used to."

Staying Out Late

Many teenagers disagree with their parents about curfews. Teenagers seem to want to stay out very late for many reasons. Joy thinks it is because they don't want to go home and they enjoy having fun when they stay out. She also thinks that some kids might not get along with their parents and come home late so that they won't get in contact with them. Nathan thinks that some teens stay out very late because they feel they are responsible enough to live their own lives. Macy thinks that some stay out late to be rebellious and to show that they are independent.

We know that parents get worried and angry when kids are out past their curfew. We've made a list of the fantasies that must go on in parents' heads about what their kids are doing if they are not home at the proper time. We think they wonder if their kids are:

doing drugs
getting in a car accident
hanging out in parks
getting arrested
going to porno movies
dead
being kidnaped by wicked strangers
selling dope
getting raped or mugged
drinking booze
having sex
committing crimes
going to discos
walking through the Combat Zone (red-light district)
getting lost
winding up in jail
stealing
lying in the gutter
disgracing the family name

We think that parents and teens need to talk about appropriate curfews. Teenagers should tell their parents where they are going and when they will be back. If you find that you cannot be back on time, give your parents a phone call. Parents need to be understanding and flexible about bedtimes and curfews, but they should be neither overprotective nor overflexible. It doesn't feel good at all to have a parent who just doesn't care what time you return home.

A girl we know told us, "My sister used to come in late every night. No matter how strict a curfew or how severe a punishment, she'd be late. Finally, my father and she had a long talk. I don't know what they said, but it worked." Talking is usually more helpful than punishment. Kids need to be responsible about making sure that they are home on time and letting their parents know if they will be late.

Parents need to understand that on some occasions — such as special parties, concerts, or school events — their teenager might need to stay out later than usual and they should try to be very flexible about this. If the parent has good reasons why a late curfew is not good on a certain night (school the next day, a vacation coming up), the teenager should listen and take this into account.

Cars and Driving

When you are still a kid, transportation isn't that big an issue for you, because most of the places you want to go you go with your parents. They either drive you, or walk with you, or you take public transportation together. For example, when you want to sleep over at a friend's house, your parents probably arrange to get you there and back.

This changes as kids grow up and become more independent. There are many places you want to visit without your parents. You prefer to spend more time with just your friends. This is when transportation can become a big problem.

In Massachusetts, where we live, people can get drivers' permits when they are sixteen years old and licenses at seventeen. The ages vary from state to state and in some states the age is as low as fourteen or fifteen. We think that teenagers should be able to learn to drive as soon as they are ready and that parents should talk about it and perhaps make sure that teenagers take some kind of driver's education course.

Not all families have cars and not all people really need to drive. If you live in a city with good public transportation, you might not feel the need to learn to drive. Most kids we know, however, are looking forward to driving, even if it seems a little bit scary at first.

If you do get a license and start to drive the family car, you should realize that other people use it too and that you need to work out a system so that everyone who needs the car can use it. Some kids we know get jobs and start to earn money to buy their own car (usually a used car) or even a motorcycle. One family we know makes out a weekly schedule about when each member may use the car, and they allow a little bit of flexibility for changes that might come up.

Until kids can drive and have a car to use when they need to go places, parents and kids need to talk about where the kids need to go and how they will get there. It is usually best all the way around for kids to get there on their own, but in some cases the destination is too far away, it's dark out and people don't want to get mugged, or there is no public transportation. In these cases, parents should try to help out — within reason — and kids should understand that when you become older and more independent you also have to take on more responsibilities.

Sex Education

Talking about sex with parents is embarrassing. There's no way around that. Some of us are more comfortable than others discussing sex and body changes with our parents, but at some time or other, we are all a little embarrassed about it.

Kids learn about sex in many different ways. Some people talk about sex education as something that goes on only in school and others through talks with their parents. We think sex education begins when a baby is born and that kids learn about sexuality and body changes in many ways. Here is a list of how we have learned about sex:

seeing changes on you and your friends
reading books and magazines
talking and joking with kids
watching movies
talking with parents
listening to teachers
experimenting with friends
watching television
reading graffiti
looking in a mirror

We think that parents should talk with their children about sex from an early age. Sometimes it is best to wait until kids ask questions, but sometimes it is helpful for the parent to start the discussion. We think that schools should offer sex education classes but that kids should not be forced to take them. We disagree about at what age these should be offered. Some of us think they should start in first or second grade and some of us think these classes should not start until junior high school.

It seems clear to many of us that talking with parents about sex gets harder as you get older. Jonathan said, "This might be because, as you get older, the questions involve you more." Kama told us, "It's easy when kids are young because they don't know what they're talking about and parents can lie. When kids get older it can be a lot harder because it is really embarrassing." Kate seems to agree with this, and said, "If I had to sum it all up in one word, I think talking about sex at any age is *embarrassing*."

It can be worse, however, to have parents who avoid talking about sex and are so uncomfortable that they never tell you about "the birds and the bees." If you find yourself in this situation, we bet that it does not make you feel good and makes it feel like you are not close to your parent at all. You need to find a way to try to make it easier for them to have this talk with you.

In general, we think parents should talk to kids about sex and body changes before they get to be big issues for the kids. It isn't a good idea to have one talk and end it at that. The kid might think about the chat and want to ask more questions. We think it is best if the parent or parents can find a way to feel comfortable with this topic and discuss it whenever it is on the kid's mind or whenever something specific comes up.

Here's what Elizabeth suggests if you have questions about sex or body changes and want to ask a parent about them: "If your parents are very open-minded, and discuss sex freely, then there should be no problem. Just ask them your question bluntly and you will usually get an honest opinion.

"If your parents never talk about sex, then it might be difficult. With a large amount of tact, carefully slip your question into the conversation. If you make it clear that you're not joking, then they will most likely get serious and give you satisfactory results.

"If your parents don't forbid any discussions about sex, but don't discuss it a lot, then you might want to ask another relative. An older sibling, grandparents, aunts, or uncles will do. Just use good judgment."

If you can't talk to your parent about sex and you have questions, ask a friend, a teacher, a school nurse, or go to the library and get a book out. A book that we recommend and have used in our classroom is *Changing Bodies, Changing*

Talking to a parent about sex is embarrassing.

Lives, by Ruth Bell and Members of the Teen Book Project of the Boston Women's Health Book Collective. This book talks about most of the teenage issues we can think of and also has a lot about sex and body changes. It is nice to have a copy around the house to answer any questions that might come up.

Some of us can talk to our parents about sex in general, but can't talk about some specific topics. We each made a list of what topics we can and can't talk about with our parents. Most kids can't talk to their parent about masturbation, maybe because this is a kind of sexual activity that people our age commonly have and talking about it is too embarrassing. It's even easier to talk about sexual intercourse than masturbation. Here are four of our lists:

GIRL #1: Can talk about periods, wet dreams, shaving, dating, and kissing. Can't talk about birth control, homosexuality, masturbation, sexual intercourse, breast development, nudity, going steady, and love.

BOY #1: Can talk about birth control, wet dreams, shaving, dating, intercourse, nudity, kissing, going steady, and love. Can't talk about periods, homosexuality, masturbation, and breast development.

GIRL #2: Can talk about everything except masturbation, homosexuality, sexual intercourse, nudity.

BOY #2: Can talk about periods, birth control, homosexuality, shaving, breast development, dating, sexual intercourse, nudity, kissing, going steady, and love. Can't talk about wet dreams and masturbation.

To help make talking about sex easier with parents, kids should realize that sometimes parents are as embarrassed about it as kids are. Dropping hints is helpful or talking about something that you've seen in a movie or read in a book.

Although most of us feel it is easier for girls to talk to mothers about sex and boys to talk to fathers, we've noticed that some boys feel more comfortable talking with their mothers. If you live in a single-parent family, you might find it very easy to talk to the parent you live with about sex — whether the parent is a father or a mother.

Talking about sex can make a kid feel closer to a parent. One girl in our class told us this story: "When I was about nine or ten, I found a diaphragm in my stepmother's drawer. I approached her and asked my question. She was appalled. She grabbed it from me and ran up to her room. When my father came home and found out what had happened, he explained to me what it was that I found. We have a very close relationship."

Parents should realize that refusing to talk about sex or talking about it in a way that shows they are uncomfortable, guilty, or feel weird can make a child feel less close to a parent. Talking as honestly and comfortably as possible would make a kid feel good and closer to the parent.

Alcohol and Drug Use

Today many people have pictures in their heads of eight-year-old kids doing a lot of drugs. While there probably are some kids who get into drugs at this age, most of us don't know anyone like this. In fact, most of us are having our first direct exposure to drugs and alcohol now — when we are eleven, twelve, and thirteen — and some of us won't have it until we're older and in high school.

Kids are usually first exposed to drugs and alcohol through television shows and movies. They hear about things like pot and cocaine and people getting drunk and high. They also hear announcements telling you that drugs and alcohol are bad and that you should never drink and drive. Many of us have never had a serious, unbiased, and informational conversation about drugs and alcohol. This is the kind of conversation, however, that we think kids need to have with their parents.

One of the most difficult parts of drug and alcohol use for teenagers is the role of peer pressure. It just isn't cool to be at a party where people are snorting cocaine or smoking pot and refuse to do it. You could feel immature or silly. Nathan told us about an experience he had at a party: "I was at a friend's party and it was very big — about one hundred people there. It was very late and I went in the bathroom to brush my teeth. Two guys were there snorting cocaine and they asked me if I wanted to try any. I said no and just brushed my teeth."

Kecia told us a similar story: "The only time I ever really had to make a decision about drugs was when a friend invited me to sleep over her house and go to a party with her. She told me the kids' parents were away for the weekend and that we'd have a blast. I knew about these 'blasts' and knew that there would be cocaine and liquor and that I would have to make a decision about whether she was the kind of friend I wanted to have. I told her that this was not my kind of party and hung up. I'm glad I made the decision that I did."

Some kids don't make the same decision that Kecia and Nathan did. Because they are curious about drugs, or because of peer pressure, they try the drugs. Some of them find out that drugs affect them in negative ways. Jake told us: "A kid I know got offered drugs about ten times before he took a little pot and got totally stoned. He hated the feeling of not being in control. He never touched drugs again."

Jamey told us about a friend of hers whose first experience of drugs wasn't so bad: "My friend's older sister used to smoke pot and she asked my friend if she wanted some and she didn't know what to say, so she took it. She found out that it wasn't as big a deal as she thought it was, it just gave her a headache."

We know that parents can't stop kids from drinking or using drugs. It's fairly simple for kids to have access to alcohol and drugs if they want to try them. Parents can, however, help us by talking with us about drugs and alcohol and letting us know the possible effects of using them. We'd like parents to tell us this information in as calm and unbiased a way as possible, and also to provide us with books and pamphlets on these things. With this kind of information, we can make up our own minds about whether or not to try them.

We think that the parents should make sure that their children can feel comfortable enough with them to ask questions about drugs and alcohol. Some parents think that it is best for kids to have their first drink at home. We think this is a good idea for some kids, especially when it comes to wine or beer.

The worst thing that can happen between parents and kids in this area is if the parent lets the kid know that he or she will be disowned if drugs or alcohol are used. Kids need to know that if they have problems, or make a mistake and take on something bigger than they can handle, their parents will help them get out of the mess and recognize their mistake. If you are afraid that your parent will kill you for trying drugs, you won't be able to go to them if you do try them and you get messed up. This creates a bad situation for everyone.

Career Issues

From the time we were very young, many of us were aware that our parents had a preference regarding the direction we take in our future lives — whether or not we go to college, what kind of job or career we pursue, whether we enter the military or not. But some of us have no idea of our parents' thoughts on these matters because we've never had a serious discussion about it, even though we have heard them drop things into conversations or make assumptions about what our lives will be like after we enter the real world.

Macy told us, "My parents never think twice about whether or not I'm going to college — they are sure I am going. Of course they never say what I'm going to major in. I ask them and they say, 'Oh, become a doctor or lawyer, so you can make big bucks!' I tell them that I don't want to do that and they suggest, 'Do dancing, modeling, cooking, acting, or writing, but marry someone rich!' "

We don't mind hearing our parents' expectations about our future lives, but we don't want to be pressured. Also, we understand that many people don't really make decisions about college and jobs until they are in their late teens or even later. It really is impossible for any of us to say what we're going to be now and be sure that we will still want to be that when we are older.

If your parents are pressuring you, you should explain to them calmly that their choice of jobs for you is not the same as your choice and that you would not be happy following their way. Some parents get upset by this because they want you to follow the same career that they did or they want you to take over the family business. Parents' suggestions might be taken into account as you think about what you want to do with your life, but in no way should you feel obligated to follow in your parents' footsteps.

Most kids should realize that they can make some choices about their future lives all along the way. You could enter a vocational training course in high school and then, after graduating, go to work right away. You could enter the military after college and learn some skills there. You could decide to pursue career ideas after high school, even without college. Whatever choices you make, you should keep in mind that you are allowed to change your mind and that this is your life and your decision.

Our Changing Relationship with Our Parents

Most of the issues that come up between teenagers and parents make it clear that a changing relationship takes place during adolescence. We talked about the different relationships we could have with our parents during this time of our life. Parents could choose to continue to have a strictly parent-child relationship, just like they had when we were five years old. But this might be difficult, since most teenagers want more independence and would like to see that their parents trust and respect them as they get older. You could have a friend-friend relationship, which is almost equal and means that the parent is more like a best friend to you. Your parent wouldn't set many limits on you at all and would be most helpful to you in talking about your life and helping you with the mistakes. This works with some kids; other kids are not responsible enough to handle it.

We think that teenagers and parents need to develop their own kind of relationships during the teenage years. If you have had a parent-child relationship based on trust and respect, we expect that it will develop as you get older and that you will become more independent. We also expect that communication between parent and teen will continue.

This is the most important message of our book: Communication between parent and child is the most important part of the relationship. Regardless of how old you are, you need to be able to talk to your parent honestly and openly and without fear. You also need to be able to listen to your parent, without being defensive and hostile. If parents and children can communicate well, almost any problem can be dealt with in an honest and helpful way. This will make children feel respected and intelligent and will make parents realize that they can learn something from their children.

We wonder if we won't feel differently about all of this in five or six years, when we are eighteen and nineteen years old. Right now, however, we feel that the relationship between parents and teens can and should be one of the most important relationships of your life and that teenagers should take some responsibility for making sure the relationship works out all right.